*Insightful, Truthful, Cha Indigenous Faith* teachir reconfirm the truth and ac... fulness of His servants - Craig and LaDonna Smith.

>Mr. Marshall M. Murdock (*Fisher River Cree Nation*)
>Indigenous Businessman
>Winnipeg, Manitoba Canada

As I read *Indigenous Faith*, I sensed a lot of blood, sweat and tears behind the words. Since I have the privilege of the author being a close personal friend, I know that it comes from a heart that cares compassionately, a mind that thinks deeply and a soul that agonizes honestly. From the point of context, the issue is documented with integrity, the premise is articulated factually and the pathway towards arriving at syncretism is explained historically. Most importantly, the criteria for evaluating the issue is placed solidly on the absolute truth of Scripture. Any open-minded advocate of syncretism is left with the reality that their argument is not with the author, but with Holy Writ. It is a work that will greatly aid the honest learner and undoubtedly will stand the test of time.

>Rev. Jay Letey
>Founder, Church Coach Ministries, Inc.
>Phoenix, Arizona

Craig is a good friend with a great heart for the Lord. He raises a very important topic for everyone interested in Christian missions among Indigenous peoples. This is an essential read for people processing the intersection of Native culture and Christian living.

>Dr. Ryan O'Leary (*Bois Forte Band of Ojibwe*)
>Professor, Leech Lake Tribal College
>Bemidji, Minnesota

In *Indigenous Faith* Craig Smith wrestles with questions about Christ and culture that are and will be live ones for Native American believers in Jesus. While not a student of Native cultures of our land, I happily applaud Craig's high view of Scriptural authority as foundational to the pursuit of critical contextualization. This is an important call for those who name Christ, not only among Native Americans, but in all of our cultures.

Rev. Tim Crouch
Vice President - International Ministries
The Christian and Missionary Alliance (US)
Colorado Springs, Colorado

I have heard Craig's presentation and to me it is very convincing. How can a person not see these truths? Check out the Scriptures that are used. God uses His Word for *correction and instruction* (11 Timothy 3:16). I recommend this book for all believers and especially for those in a position of leadership.

Pastor Bill Jackson
(*Whitefish Lake Cree Nation #128*)
Co-founder, Native Evangelical Fellowship of Canada
Goodfish Lake, Alberta Canada

To borrow from C.S. Lewis, "When the whole world is running toward a cliff, he who is running in an opposite direction appears to be the one who has lost his mind," In this poignant treatise Indigenous leader Craig Smith resists today's syncretism currents in North America and around the world and offers compelling reasoning for adhering to sound hermeneutics while adapting our methods to further the gospel message among Indigenous Peoples. Chapters 9 and 10 alone are worth the price of the book!

Rev. Dan Woodard
First Nations Ministries Facilitator Action Canada
Carstairs, Alberta Canada

*Indigenous Faith* is a valuable contribution to the contextualization/redeeming of culture discussion being addressed in global outreach efforts today. Craig's years of experience in ministry, relationships with Native First Nations people, and his deep reliance on God's Word is uplifting, convicting, and reflective in each chapter written. His questions and observations penetrate much deeper than the surface of one's culture to the heart and value of one's identity as a follower of Jesus Christ. *Indigenous Faith* is a must read for every tribe and nation today!

Rev. Huron Claus (*Mohawk/Kiowa*)
President, CHIEF, Inc.
Phoenix, Arizona

Craig Smith writes with a compassionate heart of a third generation Ojibwe Native American Christian who has a deep concern about drift from biblical orthodoxy among many indigenous people groups in North America. *Indigenous Faith* is a clarion call to clearly understand the challenges of syncretism and how to correct course. Craig's experience as evangelist, teacher, leader and pastor is evident as he describes *biblical identity and significance must take precedence over cultural identity and significance*. The book is an understandable resource for indigenous leaders, higher education faculties, and all evangelical mission leaders as they face devastating heresies such as the growing movement *Redeeming the Culture* among indigenous groups. I recommend this timely book which is easily read and skillfully presents the importance of the authoritative Word of God and the work of the Holy Spirit as the touchstones for developing an orthodox faith and church life among all people groups.

Dr. Gary Benedict
Former President of Crown College
Former President of The Christian and Missionary Alliance
(U.S) Chaska, Minnesota

While focusing on spiritual issues facing indigenous Native Americans, this book is a must read for anyone from any culture searching for Truth. This book brings into focus how past beliefs, teachings, or even personal opinions can lead us away from the remarkable goodness God has for each of us. Read this book and you will experience a new or renewed appreciation for the gift Christ has extended to all of us regardless of our background and heritage. Craig has captured the remarkable history of indigenous people while using the message of Scripture to point us all to an incredible future.

> Dr. Robert M. Myers, D.B.A.
> President, Toccoa Falls College
> Toccoa, GA

*Indigenous Faith* is perhaps the most comprehensive book ever written regarding our faith in Christ and the importance of biblical discernment in light of an indigenous cultural worldview! Utilizing key Scriptural insight combined with Rev. Smith's decades of ministerial experience, *Indigenous Faith* will provide an unparalleled look on how to distinguish and balance cultural characteristics in light of God's Word. A thorough resource for Indigenous people, non-Native leadership, and biblical scholars in higher Christian education.

> Torrey J. Antone (*Oneida First Nation*)
> Executive Director, American Indian Crusade
> Host, *Living Hope Today*, AICTV
> Oklahoma City, OK

The Great Commission directs Christ followers to make disciples of all nations. In fulfillment of that mission identifying the boundary between biblical contextualization and unbiblical syncretism is one of our greatest challenges. Grounded firmly in Scripture, Craig Smith not only succeeds in identifying that boundary, but also charts a course for ministry leaders that respects culture, retains biblical fidelity, and exalts the supremacy of Christ above all cultures. A must read for leaders navigating the complexity of intercultural ministry.

Dr. Martin Giese
President, Oak Hills Christian College
& Oak Hills Fellowship
Bemidji, MN

*Indigenous Faith* is a must read for everyone who is discerning of God's call in Native North America. Once you have begun reading this book, you will be simply unable to put it down! You will find this author's *quiet voice* has relevance and immediacy to the challenges in the North American Native context. Truth never changes, but while attempts are made to proclaim it to cultures around the world, those attempts must always be aligned with God's Word to make it relevant. Author Craig Stephen Smith combines both insight and foresight, and his work will retain a lasting validity that can be studied and restudied.

Rev. John E. Maracle, (*Mohawk, Wolf Clan*)
Chief/President, Native American
Fellowship of the Assemblies of God
Executive Presbyter,
Assemblies of God Ethnic Fellowships
Phoenix, Arizona

# Indigenous Faith

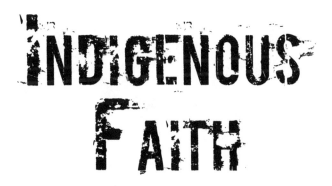

Living a biblically healthy life in the context of an indigenous culture...

**Craig Stephen Smith**

XULON PRESS

Xulon Press
2301 Lucien Way #415
Maitland, FL 32751
407.339.4217
www.xulonpress.com

© 2019 by Craig Stephen Smith

All rights reserved solely by the author. The author guarantees all contents are original and do not infringe upon the legal rights of any other person or work. No part of this book may be reproduced in any form without the permission of the author. The views expressed in this book are not necessarily those of the publisher.

Unless otherwise indicated, Scripture quotations taken from the Holy Bible, New International Version (NIV). Copyright © 1973, 1978, 1984, 2011 by Biblica, Inc.™. Used by permission. All rights reserved.

Printed in the United States of America.

ISBN-13: 978-1-54566-739-2

# DEDICATION

THIS BOOK IS DEDICATED TO THE MEMORY OF THE THREE men of God who influenced and impacted my life in ways beyond measure.

First is my father, Raymond J. Smith *(Ojibwe)*. What a privilege to have been raised by such a humble and godly man. My father has been an incredible inspiration to me while modeling godliness and character worthy to be emulated. He was not a seeker of the spotlight, though at times the spotlight sought him. He chose rather to come alongside others, supporting family and colleagues with his God given gifts of helps and service. I miss him greatly and long for the day when we will be reunited in heaven.

Also, I dedicate this work to the memory of my father-in-law, Rev. Herman J. Williams *(Navajo)*, of whom I am equally privileged to be grafted into his family's lineage. Herman's own amazing and oft' times humorous life story and faith made him unique among his peers. I learned so much about life, ministry, and faith from this man who impacted so many Christ followers in his tribe and beyond. He knew how to confront the powers of darkness through the biblical authority of the believer. It was a joy to serve together with him for so many years.

Finally, I dedicate this work to the memory of another great man of God, Rev. H. Thomas Claus *(Mohawk/Tuscarora)*. Tom was like a *third father* to me. Throughout his life he was an encourager, prayer warrior, and great blessing. We shared a mutual calling and gifting (that of the evangelist), and I learned many lessons of faith through this wonderful mentor. We became especially close in the latter part of his life after my near fatal auto accident in 2009. He would often call, visit, and encourage me in my school of suffering. It was Tom who sat by my bedside, reading the Scriptures to me, and challenging me to ponder the truths of God's Word anew. It was Scriptures such as Psalms 57:1-2 that settled the issues about God's sovereignty and love for me even in the midst of the disaster I was facing.

Great men of God are hard to come by, especially those who are willing to give of themselves in constant love, service, and encouragement to others.

Though not perfect men, these three leaders stand out as those I desire to be like. They held to the same theological principles and convictions that I seek to articulate in this painful but necessary work before you. It is to their memory, and with deep love and appreciation for them, that I dedicate *Indigenous Faith*.

# TABLE OF CONTENTS

*Foreword* .................................................. xv
*Introduction* ........................................... xxiii

## PART 1 - DEFINING THE ISSUES

Chapter 1:   Setting the Table ........................... 3
Chapter 2:   Contending for the Faith .................... 11
Chapter 3:   Building a Solid Theological Foundation ... 22
Chapter 4:   Whose Truth is Truth? ...................... 53
Chapter 5:   No Other Option ............................ 70

## PART 2 - DISCOVERING THE TRUTH

Chapter 6:   The Biblical Anatomy of Culture ........... 87
Chapter 7:   Lessons from Ezekiel ..................... 117
Chapter 8:   The "Come Down" Kingdom ................. 153

## PART 3 - DEVELOPING THE STRATEGY

Chapter 9:   What to Surrender, What to Keep ........ 187
Chapter 10: Addressing the Implications ............. 210
Chapter 11: My Game Changer Moment .............. 235

# FOREWORD

**IT TOOK A LOT OF HOLY COURAGE AND LOVING PASSION** for Craig Smith to write this crossroads book. I'm honored to call him friend.

When Craig introduces me to a Native audience, he humorously says (of a guy as white as can be), *Ron actually IS Native American...he's just been sick!*

It is, in fact, many Native friends like Craig who have introduced me to their people across this land. And I will thank God for all eternity that they have.

Growing up in Chicago, working with young people in and around New York City, and speaking with young people around the world, my life has been a multi-cultural adventure. But you don't meet many Native people in these kinds of places.

Nearly thirty years ago, my ministry took me to a reservation to speak. It was a decisive week in my life. I haven't been the same since!

I loved the people I met. My heart ached for the pain and grief they carried from centuries of loss. I was amazed by the resilient strength that enabled them to survive the loss of their land, their language, their lifestyle – and so many of their loved ones' lives. I could not shake the tragedy of so many fresh graves – many the graves of young lives snuffed out way too early.

I saw how their sense of humor often defies their pain. It has given them a unique ability to survive so much tragedy. I admired their warrior spirit and their ability to read a heart.

Since those days, my late wife and I have had the privilege of being welcomed into enriching friendships with Native brothers and sisters. They have looked past our skin and into our heart.

When our son gave us the treasure of a Navajo daughter-in-love (oh, and three Navajo grandchildren), we have been blessed beyond measure (including her irresistible frybread!) And as we have had the honor of ministering with inter-tribal teams on over a hundred reservations and reserves, we gained an extended family of hundreds of native *sons* and *daughters*.

We have seen them share the hope they have found in Jesus with an effectiveness that can only be attributed to the power of God poured through a willing and often-broken vessel.

Their boldness, their willingness to leave their comfort zone, and their tears for their people are a powerful example for the rest of God's people. The warrior spirit of a First Nations person, unleashed under the leadership of Jesus Christ, is something mighty to see! I have been

*Foreword*

humbled by their praying, challenged by their courage and ignited by their passion.

I have also seen how relentlessly the enemy of our souls bombards them with attacks designed to deceive, to distract, to derail them. Satan knows how much he has to lose if they follow God's orders to *do your best to present yourself to God as one approved, a workman that does not need to be ashamed and who correctly handles the word of truth* (2 Timothy 2:15).

My heart breaks when I see these walking miracles struggle. Not only with the temptations of their past, but with the questions raised by being both Native and a Jesus-follower. It is a struggle for every committed believer in every generation, in every culture.

Thankfully, God has not left us adrift when it comes to discerning His will and His way. In His final known prayer for His followers, Jesus prayed, *Sanctify them by the truth; Your word is truth* (John 17:17). And the Apostle John warns us: *Do not believe every spirit, but test the spirits to see whether they are from God* (I John 4:1).

God's revealed Word is always the truth we can trust.

*All Scripture is inspired by God and is useful to teach what is true and to make us realize what is wrong in our lives. It corrects us when we are wrong and teaches us to do what is right. God uses it to prepare and equip His people to do every good work* (II Timothy 3:16 – NLT).

Even a cursory skimming of this book will show that Craig Smith is a man of the Word. *Indigenous Faith* is a labor of Craig's love for his Savior and his people, providing biblical guidance with singular clarity and depth. He has taken the time and had the heart to assemble what is probably the most thorough Scriptural research and analysis available on these issues.

A word about Craig. He's the real deal.

We met Craig in the beginning days of our work with Native Americans. He mentored us. He challenged us. He has made us laugh. And Craig has made us think, too. About mistakes non-Native Christian workers make with his people. About our own cultural blind spots. About some enlightening insights from God's Word, filtered through his experience as a Native man.

And Craig has made us better. During the years he directed our ministry's *On Eagles' Wings* work with Native youth, he raised the bar and deepened our impact on those precious young warriors.

He is so worth reading, listening to, learning from.

He knows his people – he has ministered among tribes across the continent. He has a proven history of raising up and training young Native Americans to become leaders for their people. And he and LaDonna's vibrant faith continues to be reflected in their children and grandchildren, who seek to follow Christ in their generations.

*Foreword*

Craig also has the expensive credentials of an overcomer. After an automobile accident he and LaDonna barely survived, he was left with a body that is tragically broken. He has endured around forty surgeries and painful procedures and continues to struggle physically with a life greatly limited by irreparable damage. And yet he continues to serve his Savior and his people with a faith made stronger and more vibrant through suffering. Wherever he goes, he brings great faith and joy.

And he remains fully engaged in ministering to his people in times like these.

The battle for the hearts of Native people – those who follow Christ and those who don't – is real, intense and now. And it is eternally important.

It is my deep conviction that the First People of this continent have a special place in God's plans to *pour out His Spirit on all flesh* (Acts 2:17). Their story is known around the world. They are listened to because of what they have suffered.

I remember Craig telling me about being asked to speak at a national church conference in Australia. After flying many hours, Craig, his wife LaDonna, and his father Ray (the Smith Family Trio), arrived in the middle of the night in southwestern Australia.

The next day, Craig preached and included a historical overview of missionary work in the United States among Native American people. When Craig finished speaking, he was like a magnet for those Aboriginal believers. With many in tears, they clustered around him. They stayed and stayed, embracing him as one of their own.

*You have told our story, you are just like us*, one believer shared through tears. An American missionary pulled Craig aside and said, *You arrived hours ago and preached one sermon. In that time, you have gotten to the heart of the Aborigines in a way I have tried to for more than twenty-five years!*

In breakthrough moments like that, and the many I have seen God pour out on reservations through His young Native warriors, the spiritual impact of Indigenous People is clear. May many others move to the front-lines of the battle as we all seek together to fulfill Jesus' Great Commission. Because of what they have lived, because of what they have lost, because of what they have overcome, reborn Native Americans are uncommon messengers of a living Christ.

It's no wonder evangelist Billy Graham observed some forty years ago:

> *The greatest moments of Native history may be ahead of us if a great spiritual renewal and awakening should take place. The Native American has been a sleeping giant. He is awakening. The original Americans could become the evangelists who will help win America for Christ! Remember these forgotten people.*

*Foreword*

We are living in decisive times. The need has never been greater. The time has never been shorter. The *reach the world orders* of Jesus have never been more urgent.

The Original People of this land are biographically credentialed and spiritually wired to play a strategic role in turning a generation to Jesus. If their Gospel is uncompromised and unencumbered. That's why making sure Indigenous faith is biblical faith is so eternally important. And that's the reason for this book.

The First Nations of this continent waited a long time for the Hope that is Jesus. And to make their mark, in Jesus' Name, on a world starved for hope.

And now, with God's blessing – finally . . . their time has come.

Ron Hutchcraft
Radio Host of A Word with You daily broadcast
Public Speaker
Author of Hope When Your Heart Is Breaking
President, Ron Hutchcraft Ministries
Founder, On Eagles' Wings (Hope for Native America)

# INTRODUCTION

*No prophet of God can neglect his times; but the work of the prophet is not to devise a message from the imagination of his heart. After observation of the times, the work of the prophet is to declare the Word of God to the times for their correction. We, who are the Christian ministry, are sometimes told, that what we need in order to be successful is to catch the spirit of the age. Nothing of the kind; Our work is to correct the spirit of the age, and never to catch it; to know it, and to correct it.*
Dr. G. Campbell Morgan

**IT HAS BEEN OVER TWO THOUSAND YEARS SINCE A SMALL** group of Christ followers stood gazing toward the heavens, watching as the risen Christ ascended back to His rightful place at the right hand of God the Father. Just before His feet left earth, Christ gave them His final words as recorded in Acts 1:8.

*But you will receive power when the Holy Spirit comes on you; and you will be my witnesses in Jerusalem, and in all Judea and Samaria, and to the ends of the earth.*

With those words in hand, this small group of Christ followers once again felt, no doubt, the pain they experienced less than a month and a half prior, when they saw Christ die on the cross. But this time, something was different. Today's pain was the sting of the most influential person who ever lived not being there in person anymore to lead the charge of the commission He had just given them to fulfill. The effects of His glorious resurrection, however, surely tempered that pain. They knew Jesus was a man who kept His word for they were with Him, the risen Lamb of God, for some forty additional life-impacting days. They had His assurance that He would come back again, a promise we still anxiously await to this very day!

This all-encompassing commission was not to be interpreted by those who heard it as a *pick the one you want* imperative. Christ's followers ever since then have been charged with an all-inclusive global mandate. We've got to be *all in* until Christ returns!

With the reality of losing their leader fresh on their mind, no doubt some of the more skeptical and weaker of faith may have thought, *Yeah, you give us this command and right after you tell us what to do - you leave! How on earth are we going to do this?*

*Introduction*

It is wonderful to know that before Jesus uttered this last command to *go*, He first told them to *stay*. Acts 1:4-5 notes;

*On one occasion, while he was eating with them, he gave them this command: "Do not leave Jerusalem, but wait for the gift my Father promised, which you have heard me speak about. For John baptized with water, but in a few days you will be baptized with the Holy Spirit."*

Since the arrival of the Holy Spirit on the day of Pentecost, this handful of believers has grown into a worldwide movement estimated at 2.5 billion strong. Approximately one-third of the world's population claims to be followers of Christ.

While true that not all people who claim to be Christians are born again followers of Christ, it can't be denied that something significant has taken place in world history. So many people, from so many diverse places, have taken up the banner of the cross and are faithfully following the One *whom we have not yet seen.*

I am glad they got the staying part down before they ever tried to do the going part. The ascension of Christ paved the way for the third member of the Trinity, the Holy Spirit, to come down from above and fill the early believers with power from on high. His coming gave birth to the Church of the Risen Christ, enabling them to preach the gospel in languages of the many tribes assembled in Jerusalem on the day of Pentecost.

On opening day of the Church, it grew exponentially from 120 to well over 3,000 people! From that day to this day, the power of the Holy Spirit is still the dependable source of strength and enabling as the Church continues to do the going part.

Those commanding words of Christ to go into all the world implies that throughout its history, and as it moves forward into the future, the Church must continue to cross cultures until every tribe, language, people, and nation, are presented with the gospel of Jesus Christ.

There are some obvious and important questions the Church needs to ask itself as it seeks to be obedient to the command to go.

Are we clearly articulating the primary message Christ wants us to proclaim? How do we enter another culture and bring a message that is not the basis of belief for that culture? How do we share the one and only message that can transform not only an individual, but impact a whole culture as well?

These questions continue to be looked at by missiologists and churchmen alike. These are all important pursuits. I am often left to wonder, however, if those questions arise because we are missing the dynamic *power from on high.* That may be a simplistic statement, but the intent of this book has that emphasis in mind.

*Introduction*

By staying, I am not suggesting we go and re-enter an upper room and wait for another Pentecost experience where cloven tongues of fire come in and visit the room. That visitation was a unique, one-time event that marked the birth of the Church.

It is good to know that the Spirit came to earth at Pentecost, and has not left! The Holy Spirit continues to be available to us today as we seek to, in our generation, fulfill the Great Commission. The imperative continues, *be filled with the Holy Spirit!*

The true way of the cross will never be a popular message to proclaim. It challenges us to make subordinate every vestige of personal and cultural identity, significance, and importance, to what Paul found to be *the surpassing greatness of knowing Christ*. A denying one's self message will never win the popular vote, nor draw those wanting to live as close to the old sin nature as possible.

*Indigenous Faith* will challenge opinions and views on how we are to live our lives in the context of the Word of God and is applicable to any earthly culture and worldview. Of specific importance is how the gospel can and must impact people raised in the context of indigenous cultures with animistic belief systems.

In my first book, *Whiteman's Gospel,* (Indian Life Books), originally published in 1997, I put forward a response to an issue that was beginning to surface at the time in Native ministry. It pertained to lines that were, in my opinion, beginning to be crossed between proper and healthy critical contextualization (the process of putting the gospel message in a way another culture can understand and be influenced by it), and unintended or even blatant syncretism (the attempt to blend or mix the gospel with the traditional religion of the people group attempting to be reached).

I noted,

> *We must be careful, however, not to make an equally damaging mistake, in a reactionary way, to the mistakes of the past. In our efforts to make Christ more palatable to Native people, we are tempted to move in the opposite direction by embracing the lost, or previously thrown out elements, of our old Native sin-stained cultures. In doing so, we run the risk of pursuing a rebirth of old animism, masquerading as a more cultural expression and form of Christian worship and faith. In our desire to have Christ "look more Indian," enthusiasm could blind us to spiritual sensitivity. The line must be drawn on what is permissible and what is clearly defined in Scripture as against the principles of the Kingdom of God.*[1]

In June of 2009, my wife and I were involved in a near fatal, life-altering, automobile accident. God in His great mercy spared both our lives. Neither of us, humanly speaking, should be alive today. It was nothing short of a

---

[1] Whiteman's Gospel, p.124, Indian Life Books

miracle of God. We continue to suffer the consequences in very broken bodies. We are living on borrowed time, and that fact alone is a great motivator for us to address these issues in written form. As old as I now find myself, and living with these ongoing physical challenges, I realize that there are a lot more days behind me than ahead of me.

I trust and pray that my heart on these matters will come through clearly and simply, and that these thoughts will long outlast my own human earthly experience.

As we await the imminent return of Jesus Christ, the world still stands in the need of a Savior. The power of Christ alone can eternally change a person. He is also the only One sufficient enough to transform a whole nation or tribe!

To that end, may these thoughts help indigenous people around the globe, and those that seek to bring the gospel to them, find life abundant and encouragement sufficient to persevere in the new life Christ died to give us!

Craig Stephen Smith
White Earth Band of Ojibwe

# PART 1
# DEFINING THE ISSUES

*Chapter One*

# SETTING THE TABLE

THE BACK-PAGE ADVERTISEMENT WAS IMPRESSIVE. IT was colorful, dramatic, and artistically appealing. The ad was promoting an upcoming pow-wow where all the ingredients of a traditional Native pow-wow were to be included. There would be drumming, dancing, and all the colorful regalia that would be found in just about every such gathering around Native North America.

This advertisement was widely distributed as the Native paper carrying it had long established a national and international distribution network.

But the gathering being promoted was much different from the routine pow-wow events that fill the calendars of most Native tribes where Native spirituality is woven deeply and intricately into every fabric of traditional cultural events. The sponsor of this event was not a tribal government or some other typical group. This pow-wow was billed as a "Christian Pow-wow" and was sponsored by a new Native ministry organization that was emerging on the evangelical Native ministry scene in the mid-1990's.

This particular event is symbolic and representative of a major doctrinal shift in the past few decades as to what evangelical ministry organizations would sponsor or endorse as inclusive of their faith, positions, and practices.

Missiologists have been hard pressed to offer thoughtful and biblically based opposition or challenge to this movement, in fear, I think, of offending the Native leaders who have been at the forefront of this new philosophy. On the contrary, these Native leaders have been receiving warm receptions in many of the halls of higher Christian academia as they seek to reshape the thinking of the next generation of Christian leaders, ministers, and missionaries.

The current political and cultural climate in North America is such that opposition to any minority group's positions or statements, for whatever reason, is at least uncomfortable, if not downright dangerous. Blaming America's dominant society for all of America's ills continues to be a popular movement in the early years of the 21st Century.

Historical orthodoxy and positions of many Bible believing churches, denominations, and mission organizations are being publicly challenged by some of the more vocal Native leaders in this movement. Remarkably, those sharp criticisms of the larger Body of Christ have actually resulted in an awkwardly enthusiastic acceptance in churches across the land. An opening of the wallets from

God's mesmerized and guilt-ridden people often occur right after being the recipient of a fairly severe missiological tongue lashing. This has helped further this and other like-minded organizations and their purposes, enabling an expanded promotion of this teaching.

What isn't understood as much, though, is the fact that not all evangelical indigenous Christian leaders, including myself, have bought into this new doctrinal perspective and paradigm shift in methodologies. There is a band of like-minded leaders who have stood consistently opposed to this teaching as it has attempted to make its way into the congregations to which we have oversight.

In the North American indigenous context, culture and spirituality is not compartmentalized as it is in Western culture. Native culture and spirituality coexist as mutually necessary towards completing each other's working self-definitions. To a traditional North American Native person, spirituality *is* our culture, and our culture *is* our spirituality. Even the smallest of everyday things and activities can have significant spiritual implications.

Its closest parallel can be found within Christian faith and teaching. True Christ followers are called by God to consider everything we do to be done for the glory of God.

*And whatever you do, whether in word or deed, do it all in the name of the Lord Jesus, giving thanks to God the Father through him.* Colossians 1:17.

But that is where the comparisons stop. Christian faith is different from the spirituality associated with *any* human culture. The lines between the two are being blurred when something other than biblical truth defines what Christian spirituality is for us as indigenous people.

That is why my heart has been heavy about addressing this issue, without compromise, from the only source of true spirituality, God's Holy Word. When you have been in Native ministry as long as I have, you consistently maintain a very broken heart because of the lack of response of your people to the only hope available that can liberate a soul. I often feel like the Old Testament prophet, Jeremiah, who describes my broken heart as much as he does his when he says in Jeremiah 9:1;

> *Oh, that my head were a spring of water and my eyes a fountain of tears! I would weep day and night for the slain of my people.*

Native work, in and of itself, is challenging. We now have had to add to the mix a new battlefront. It is the battle against new methodologies of compromise that have made their way into evangelicalism that can seem more appealing because they incorporate the gospel *into the spiritualities born out of fallen human nature and cultures.* That makes the heartache within me only deepen.

I love my people with all my heart. I grieve when the enemy of our souls manifests his mayhem in our communities through violence, abuses of all sorts, rampant drug use and abuse, and, as my dear friend Ron Hutchcraft describes, *so many fresh graves.*

The hope that I have found through Jesus Christ has been the most powerful thing in my life. Transforming me, forgiving me, and even empowering me to live and love life unencumbered by even the physical limitations that often destroy people and cause them to be angry with God. The *peace that passes all understanding* (Philippians 4:7) is a daily experience for me, and I long to see more of my people experience all the fullness Christ offers if they'd only turn to Him, accept His free gift of salvation, and live with a new found hope for eternity!

That's why I love God's Word so much, and am so passionate to uphold its truths when they are being compromised by those who Scriptures say, carry with them *every wind of doctrine* (Ephesians 4:14) that is contrary to solid biblical truth.

This book is a clarion call to return to the authority of Scripture for believers in Jesus Christ. I trust you will have an open mind and heart to understand what the issues are, what the Word of God has to say, and then respond in obedience to the promptings of the Holy Spirit.

This self-named phenomenon known as *Redeeming the Culture* has been incredibly surprising to observe as it has played itself out over these past few decades. It is what I was referring to in *Whiteman's Gospel* as noted in the introduction of this book. I wrote those words of caution as this movement was just beginning to push its way into evangelical Native ministry in the mid to late 1990's.

One of the headlines contained in the pow-wow ad was that attendees of this *Christian Pow-wow* would be able to experience *culturally appropriate worship.* The whole theme was to experience the *redeeming of the Native American culture.* This statement alone raises a key question in my mind. That question is, *How does a fallen human culture determine what is appropriate Christian worship?* Is not appropriate Christian faith and practice determined solely by the inerrant Scriptures? When did things change in Christianity where *cultural relevance* so blatantly replaced *biblical revelation?*

Non-native people often have a romanticized view of our indigenous cultures with its pageantry, color, and spirituality. What often is not understood is the dark side of animism and its dependence on the supernatural. Fear is often the motivator for those in animistic worship. Appeasing the spirits who can and do bring harm to a family is a costly endeavor, not only financially, but emotionally, and spiritually as well.

Because of this misguided romanticism and blindness to animism's dark side, it makes it easier to understand how non-native Christians would embrace this movement. Who wouldn't support Native Christian people expressing the cultural traditions and ways unique to them in their newfound relationship with Christ?

It is a popular message in a world that now disparages, with ever increasing hostility, the dominate society in America and its historical ways of dealing with the other cultures it finds itself living and ministering among.

It is the perfect storm of cultural conflict and false doctrine that is easily acceptable and convenient to embrace. It has been fueled because the Christian community is moving further away from its biblical anchor in historic orthodoxy,[2] resulting in an altered orthopraxy,[3] that under scrutiny cannot be supported by those abandoned moorings. This perfect storm produces, inevitably, a vicious cycle. It starts with an abandonment of the authority of Scripture, disparages the messengers of the gospel, begins to let other than biblical sources serve as authoritative measuring rods of acceptable practices, which then results in less than biblical worship and godly living. It eventually leads to a trip down the broad road of syncretism. One becomes convinced that it is the right thing to do.

Truth becomes relative. Instead of Scripture having rightful authority over every human culture, the table is turned upside down as each cultural community now exercises primacy over the Scriptures. Culture now seeks to

---

[2] *Belief in an accepted doctrine.*

[3] *Practice or action based on orthodoxy.*

mold and shape Christianity's message and practices into its own fallen nature.

It is in this very environment we now find ourselves in. More than ever before, godly leaders must stand together in affirmation of biblical truth that guides and informs all aspects of Christian faith and practice. While never popular, it is of utmost importance.

Where do you stand, my friend, when someone comes to your church bringing a message that doesn't line up with biblical doctrine? With a heavy heart, I cannot stand by in silence but must proclaim the timeless truths of God's Holy Word. To do otherwise would be a dereliction of my duties as a minister of the gospel.

*Chapter Two*

## CONTENDING FOR THE FAITH

> Jude 1:3; *Dear friends, although I was very eager to write to you about the salvation we share, I felt compelled to write and urge you to contend for the faith that was once for all entrusted to God's holy people.*

CONTENDING FOR THE FAITH IS BASED ON JUDE'S important admonition found in verse 3 of this short Epistle. It is an especially important call to maintain truth for those who seek to cross cultures in bringing the gospel to lost people around the globe.

The author is Jude, the brother of James, both of whom were half-brothers of Jesus Christ. It would be a great understatement to note Jude and James had a different father than that of their unique sibling, Jesus the Christ! It reminds me of a great country gospel song titled, *On My Father's Side.*

It goes like this;

*Just a young boy in the temple one day,*
*shared with the doctors they were so amazed,*
*never had they seen one so young speak so swift,*
*they asked him many questions the conversation*
*went like this*

*Chorus:*
*What's your name son? On my mother's side my name is Jesus,*
*but on my father's side they call me Emmanuel,*
*How old are you? On my mother's side now I'm twelve years,*
*but on my father's side I've just always been,*
*Where are you from? On my mother's side I'm from Bethlehem,*
*but on my father's side it's new Jerusalem,*
*What's your plan? On my mother's side I'll be crucified,*
*but on my father's side in three days I'll arise and I'll sit at my father's side.*

*Verse: 2*
*He was the Son of God yet the son of man,*
*and I can't help but wonder how Joseph must have felt,*
*through an open door that day he heard his son reply,*

*he said, You see I'm the King of kings, that's on my father's side.*[4]

Jude wrote this letter to address false teaching and to illustrate a contrast between the error of heresy and the truth of Jesus Christ. This book has only one chapter and his teaching is divided into two parts.

In verses 1-16, Jude identifies himself and quickly delves into the dilemma of false teaching. *For certain persons have crept in unnoticed* (v. 4). Heresy was obviously seeping into the region, disturbing the churches, and deceiving believers.

In verses 17-25, Jude urges Christians to, *Remember the words that were spoken beforehand by the apostles of our Lord Jesus Christ* (v.17). He was referring to all of the apostles and disciples in the past, which had warned about false teachers and prophets that were coming to deceive. He admonished his readers to focus on Christ and to watch out for each other so that no one be misled into error.

This was a great admonition then and still is a great admonition for us today. It serves as the foundational truth for how we, as indigenous followers of Jesus Christ, must live.

Several things stand out to me from this verse.

First, It is a *shared salvation.* Christianity is not an endorsement of a potluck of religions, one for each tribe

---

[4] ©1981 Dayspring Music, LLC (a division of Word Music Group, Inc.). Words and music by *Felicia Shiflett.*

that *God has given*. Contrarily, it stands out in its exclusivity as providing a single salvation plan needed for every tribe of man! Along with that is a call to live lives in keeping with biblical doctrine and practices that the redeemed ones mutually share together, regardless of race, color, or ethnicity.

Secondly, It is a message worth *contending for.*

In its original context, the term to *contend for* implied something more than just holding a position about something. It implies a deep struggle, to pit oneself against another who tries to bring anything other than what God *originally intended to convey to the world* in His revealed Word.

Why? Because wherever there is God's truth, Satan's lies will be close behind. Error will always be nipping at the heels of the truths of God, forever seeking to replace it, or at least bring confusion to it. The enemy of God has no better plan.

We also need to remember that this is a *once for all faith!* World religions demand ongoing sacrifice. The gospel is a once for all plan, paid for by the once for all sacrifice of a once and for all Savior, Jesus Christ, some two thousand years ago!

There are two significant implications in knowing how the new life in Christ is to be lived out, in the power of the Holy Spirit, as indigenous people living in the context of our tribal cultures.

1. How I live my life individually as an indigenous Christian person.
2. How we choose to worship God and grow together corporately in the context of a healthy local church.

We often use the phrase, *I have a personal relationship with Christ*. But there is more to the Christian life than that. I not only am to have a *personal relationship* with Christ, I am called by God to have a *corporate relationship* with Him as well, lived out in the context of a healthy local church.

The teachings of the *Redeeming the Culture* movement have brought confusion to both the personal and corporate life of Native American and First Nations believers. Both issues need to be explored because they are interrelated.

One of the leaders of this contemporary movement, who has not received universal support and endorsement of Native evangelical leaders, was a man named Richard Twiss. He rose to prominence nationally in the first decade of this new millennium and passed on unexpectedly in February 2013.

In an interview with Mission Frontiers Magazine in 2010, Mr. Twiss stated the following;

> *I was made to burn and destroy all my tribal carvings, eagle feathers, and my dance outfit because the pastor told me now that I was a Christian, old things passed away and all things became new, which meant all my*

> *Native cultural ways needed to be replaced with Euro-American cultural ways. Then I was told I could no longer participate in our Native gatherings, dances or ceremonies because they were of the devil and full of idolatry. They even told me my Native drum was an idol and full of spirits, so I burned it and learned the guitar instead. Now I am no longer a Native in my culture. I am an anglicized Christian in American culture. The Bible has been used to colonize my soul.[5]*

These are strong and indicting words that help formulate the teaching this movement has been promoting for several decades. We would be wrong to believe that, with his passing, this movement has or will be diminished. We continue to hear about the *Redeeming of Culture* teaching to this day.

Richard's quote addresses the *personal relationship with Christ* issue facing indigenous people. Twiss notes the one telling him to abandon all his cultural ways was *the pastor*, implying that pastor to be a non-Native cross-cultural minister of the gospel. It is the White man once again telling the Indian what he can or cannot do.

It is also interesting to note that the pastor was instructing him to replace the Native ways with *Euro-American cultural*

---

[5] Mission Frontiers, Vol. 32, No. 5, September-October 2010, page 6, published by Frontier Ventures.

*ways.* That statement has even been attributed to me by some of the leaders in this movement.

For several decades now, my first book *Whiteman's Gospel* has been in circulation. It was even promoted in the early years by some in this movement as supportive of their teaching by misinterpreting some of the statements I put forward in that work.

In one such statement I noted;

<u>The mistake the church made among Indian people in its efforts to evangelize was when they tried to move us from our culture horizontally to their society's sin-stained culture.</u> *Those damaging efforts replaced vertical redemption where the Indian's ways were to be brought under the authority of the principles of God's Word and the higher Kingdom of God and its standards. We must be careful, however, not to make an equally damaging mistake, in a reactionary way, to the mistakes of the past. In our efforts to make Christ more palatable to Native people, we are tempted to move in the opposite direction by embracing the lost, or previously thrown out elements, of our old Native sin-stained cultures. In doing so, we run the risk of pursuing a rebirth of old animism, masquerading as a more cultural expression and form of Christian worship and faith. In our desire to have Christ "look more Indian," enthusiasm could blind us to spiritual sensitivity. The line must be drawn on what is permissible*

> and what is clearly defined in Scripture as against the principles of the Kingdom of God. <u>The statement must be made that in all cultures, there is much that is good, which can be sanctified and used in the new, higher Kingdom of God.</u> Conversely, there are things, and perhaps many things, that are contrary to the teachings of the Kingdom of God. Where and when these contrary cultural issues arise, they must be set aside for the sake of the higher Kingdom. The bottom line is, the Bible must become our guide book, and its words the final authority in the matter (emphasis added). [6]

I need to go on record and clarify the issue. It is important for me to do so as opposition to this book will undoubtedly arise from the current leaders of this movement.

Words matter! I am learning that reality as I continue my personal relationship with Christ, my role in ministry to others, and as I leave behind my thoughts and convictions through my writings. I wish I could go back in time and further develop the thoughts that this important part of *Whiteman's Gospel* states.

I have experienced my statements being pulled out of the context in which it was made and turned into statements that were never intended. Case in point are the two sentences underlined above.

---
[6] ibid, Page 124

The horizontal movement from our sin-stained culture to another that replaces the vertical redemption offered by Christ does not represent the whole of historic Native missionary efforts. I should have been clearer on that point. Yes, in *Whiteman's Gospel*, I did state that the church has been guilty at times in a horizontal redemption message, but make no mistake, my position all along has been that this wasn't always the case!

Along with the misguided missiological principles of some, there were many more cross-cultural workers who God used mightily to win, disciple, and equip Native people in victorious Christian living. Our family, among many others, are the fruit of their labors.

Also, when you read further, you note I offer sincere concern about an *equally damaging mistake, in a reactionary way, to the mistakes of the past...*and that would be the very teaching the syncretists promote today. My greatest concerns have now become reality and that breaks my heart to see. This teaching has spread in a way that drought-stricken wildfires spread.

I also want to address the other underlined sentence about the *Kingdom of God* and how it relates to this issue.

The concept of the *Kingdom of God*, as introduced in *Whiteman's Gospel*, needed much further development. If we are to understand the new life in Christ as articulated by the Word of God, we would clearly understand that the *Redeeming of Culture* movement cannot be supported biblically in any way, shape, or form. That is my strong conviction.

Effective missionaries in the past invested in solid biblical discipling of indigenous believers, of such were my grandparents. Being discipled in truth enabled them to live for Christ, not as Euro-American Christian's do, but as all nations do who desire to live in accordance with God's Word!

*Indigenous Faith* is not just a personal matter. It affects the corporate life of the believer and how we as indigenous people worship the One true Living God.

Back in the late 1990's, I was serving as the superintendent of The Native American District of The Christian and Missionary Alliance (US). Our district leadership team agreed we needed to study this new *Redeeming of Culture* teaching that was making its way into evangelical Native ministry. A task force was formed, which met for days studying the writings and transcripts of the key leaders promoting this teaching. A report was written and presented to the workers and lay leaders of our Native Alliance churches. Its findings and recommendations received unanimous approval from the delegates at our District Conference in 2000. To this day the Native Alliance congregations across the United States stand together in agreement that we will not allow this teaching in our churches.

The final report was published in a booklet titled *Boundary Lines* and has been in circulation ever since. It has served as a helpful guide to many other evangelical groups working among indigenous people here at home and around the world.

In the introductory part of *Boundary Lines*, the task force noted,

> *Recently, there has been introduced in the native evangelical church community the concept that drums, rattles, and other sacred paraphernalia formerly used in animistic worship can be "redeemed" for use in Christian worship. This position does not enjoy consensus among native evangelical church leaders.*[7]

This is the *corporate side* of *Indigenous Faith*. How do we, as indigenous people, appropriately worship God in the context of our local churches? How far can diversity go before encroaching on the boundary lines of biblical truth, or are there any boundary lines to worry about at all? Are there to be similarities in how we worship God to be found around the world or are there acceptable uniquenesses in all the diversified ways of worship many cultures bring to the worldwide Body of Christ? Important questions, for sure, and ones that need good solid biblical answers.

---

[7] Boundary Lines, Page 5

*Chapter Three*

# BUILDING A SOLID THEOLOGICAL FOUNDATION

HAVING GOOD THEOLOGY IS IMPORTANT TO LEARNING how to live out our *Indigenous Faith*. After all, when we come to faith in Christ, we are entering into a new relationship with God, our Creator, which stands in stark contrast with the traditional beliefs and practices of our unique indigenous cultures.

Our adherence to the Bible as our *only rule of Christian faith and practice* requires we examine how to live and worship God in the light of biblical doctrine. Our methods used in worship must always conform to the guidelines of Scripture. Christ taught that true worshippers worship God *in spirit and in truth* (John 4:23). Though worship has a cultural aspect, it is primarily a theological matter.[8]

As we continue to set the table, it is important to lay out some very important theological concepts that provide the foundation and framework for God-honoring *Indigenous*

---

[8] Ibid, p.8.

*Faith*, especially when lived out in the context of an animistic people group.

So, what is *animism?*

In *Boundary Lines,* The C&MA Native leadership offered the following definition of the term.

> *Animism is a religious system, and is also a philosophical system, which supplies its followers with a worldview. Animists believe that spirits indwell all animate and inanimate objects. Even those animists who believe in one superior Creator God worship the spirits and not the Creator God. Animists sometimes distinguish what they perceive to be good and evil spirits. Scholars have correctly called animism a medical system, whereby the followers depend upon the spirit world in their battle with sickness and disease.*[9]

If you were to look with us at the volumes of written materials supporting the syncretists, as our C&MA Native Theological Task Force did back in the late 1990's, you would have seen that we were being confronted with a number of misapplied key theological concepts by the early promoters of the *Redeeming the Culture* movement.

Those concepts included *Christology; Redemption; Holiness; The Church; Demonology (Power Encounter);*

---

[9] Ibid, p.6.

*Doctrines of Special Revelation and General Revelation; and Hermeneutics.*

With the gracious permission of the Native American Association of The C&MA leadership committee, the remainder of this chapter is our C&MA Native American District's position as outlined in *Boundary Lines*. It is the Task Force's statement and position regarding what we believe the Scriptures have to say about these important concepts, and also, how the *Redeeming of Culture* leaders were erroneously applying these concepts to make their case.

Keep in mind these theological concepts as we move throughout the remainder of this book. They are the foundation on which biblical *Indigenous Faith* must rest and from which I will be continually referring to as I seek to build a biblical case for truth.

## *Christology*[10]

Christology is the study of who Christ is, what He does, and His position and power. The Bible has as its central theme in both the Old and New Testaments the person of Jesus Christ, God's only begotten Son. The Old Testament is an arrow that points to the coming Christ. The New Testament tells the story of His virgin birth, sinless life, atoning sacrifice on the cross, bodily resurrection from the dead, ascension back to His Father, and His second coming. The main point of Christology

---

[10] Ibid, p.9.

is that Jesus Christ is the one and only mediator between God and man.

> I Tim. 2:5; *For there is one God and one mediator between God and men, the man Christ Jesus.*

> John 14:6; *Jesus answered, I am the way and the truth and the life. No one comes to the Father except through me.*

We affirm that outside of Jesus Christ, there is no other way to the Father/Creator, but by Him. This holds true for all generations of people since the creation of man. Obedience to the Creator by any people before a knowledge of Jesus is not enough for true salvation. There must be an expression of faith and trust in the complete work of Jesus Christ. The taking of the gospel to all nations is imperative for all nations to experience true salvation.

> Matt 24:14; *And this gospel of the kingdom will be preached in the whole world as a testimony to all nations, and then the end will come.*

Because of this foundational truth, the native believer in Jesus Christ must abandon the usage of any traditional (or contemporary) object that would serve as mediator between man and the spirit realm.

Another important aspect of Christology is the doctrine of Christ being the Head of the church, and He has given us the parameters of worship - spirit and truth.

John 4:23-24; *Yet a time is coming and has now come when the true worshipers will worship the Father in spirit and truth, for they are the kind of worshipers the Father seeks. God is spirit, and his worshipers must worship in spirit and in truth.*

True worship of Christ must be both spiritual and it must be based on truth. The Holy Spirit is the energy of worship, and the truth of God's Word is the substance of true worship. This means that no objects are necessary for true worship to take place. Objects we may elect to use in worship must conform to Christ's principles of worship.

### *Redemption*[11]

While land, time and other things are mentioned as being redeemed in Scripture, there is no record of any object used in spirit worship ever being redeemed. Theologically, the normal use of the term "redemption" in the New Testament is the deliverance of man from sin and Satan. While the New Testament does make general statements such as "redeeming

---

[11] ibid

the time", this gives no license to the concept that (sacred) objects can be redeemed.

Scripture does show, in both the Old and New Testaments, objects used in spirit worship were destroyed as an act of obedience to God.

> Acts 19:19-20; *A number who had practiced sorcery brought their scrolls together and burned them publicly. When they calculated the value of the scrolls, the total came to fifty thousand drachmas. In this way the word of the Lord spread widely and grew in power.*

> II Ki 23:6; *He took the Asherah pole from the temple of the LORD to the Kidron Valley outside Jerusalem and burned it there. He ground it to powder and scattered the dust over the graves of the common people.*

> II Ki 23:12; *He pulled down the altars the kings of Judah had erected on the roof near the upper room of Ahaz, and the altars Manasseh had built in the two courts of the temple of the LORD. He removed them from there, smashed them to pieces and threw the rubble into the Kidron Valley.*

> II Ki 23:14-15; *Josiah smashed the sacred stones and cut down the Asherah poles and covered the sites with human bones. Even the altar at Bethel, the high place made by Jeroboam son of Nebat, who had caused Israel to sin-- even*

*that altar and high place he demolished. He burned the high place and ground it to powder, and burned the Asherah pole also.*

The biblical teaching of the nature of our identity is to be found in the doctrine of redemption.

Col 1:13-14; *For he has rescued us from the dominion of darkness and brought us into the kingdom of the Son he loves, in whom we have redemption, the forgiveness of sins.*

Eph 1:5-7; *he predestined us to be adopted as his sons through Jesus Christ, in accordance with his pleasure and will--to the praise of his glorious grace, which he has freely given us in the One he loves. In him we have redemption through his blood, the forgiveness of sins, in accordance with the riches of God's grace.*

Our original identity is that of a sinner, regardless of race, socio-economic level from which we have come. The redeeming power of Christ, according to the Apostle Paul, gives to us a new identity. We are sons of God -- irrespective of what we may have been in the past. This is true for all Christians, from every tribe, tongue, and nation. Because of this new identity, we can say as the Apostle Paul says of his life,

Phil 3:4-8; *though I myself have reasons for such confidence. If anyone else thinks he has reasons to put confidence in the flesh, I have more: circumcised on the eighth day, of the people of Israel, of the tribe of Benjamin, a Hebrew of Hebrews; in regard to the law, a Pharisee; as for zeal, persecuting the church; as for legalistic righteousness, faultless. But whatever was to my profit I now consider loss for the sake of Christ. What is more, I consider everything a loss compared to the surpassing greatness of knowing Christ Jesus my Lord, for whose sake I have lost all things. I consider them rubbish that I may gain Christ.*

The foundation of our identity as believers must be a biblical identity, rather than a secular or cultural concept of identity. For the Christian, biblical identity takes precedence over any other definition of identity.

### Holiness[12]

God has no other plan for the believer but to be holy. Holiness is a part of full salvation purchased for us at such a high price by the blood of Christ. An important aspect of holiness is separation from all that displeases God.

2 Cor. 6:14-16; *Do not be yoked together with unbelievers. For what do righteousness and wickedness have*

---

[12] ibid

*in common? Or what fellowship can light have with darkness? What harmony is there between Christ and Belial? What does a believer have in common with an unbeliever? What agreement is there between the temple of God and idols? For we are the temple of the living God. As God has said: "I will live with them and walk among them, and I will be their God, and they will be my people."*

In this passage, the apostle, no less than four times, pinpoints the necessity of full separation from the works of darkness. The apostolic admonition in 2 Cor. 6:17 obligates the believer to separate himself from all forms of uncleanness. There is no suggestion that the unclean is to be cleansed, but rather, the believer is to come out of the unclean system, and not even touch the unclean thing. Obedience to this command results in the blessing of God.

The idea of redeeming objects from spirit worship for Christian worship cannot be reconciled with the biblical position on separation from such objects and practices.

2 Cor. 6:17; *Therefore come out from them and be separate, says the Lord. Touch no unclean thing, and I will receive you.*

The Scripture also distinctly connects true worship to the issue of biblical holiness.

Ps 29:2 *Ascribe to the LORD the glory due his name; worship the LORD in the splendor of his holiness.*

Ps 99:9 *Exalt the LORD our God and worship at his holy mountain, for the LORD our God is holy.*

Holiness is more than just separation. It is our union with the Holy nature of God. True worship can only be realized in the presence of our Holy God. Things of the past, present or future have no bearing on the manifestation of God. God's invitation to us is to come to His Holy hill with clean hands and a pure heart.

Ps 24:4-5; *He who has clean hands and a pure heart, who does not lift up his soul to an idol or swear by what is false. He will receive blessing from the LORD and vindication from God his Savior.*

Therefore, Christian worship is distinctly new and from God, and is not dependent on anyone's culture. Though there are different styles of worship among different people, all worship must conform to the biblical conditions and parameters for worship. They are the same for all people who come to Christ.

## The Church[13]

The concept of the New Testament Church is not a product of culture. It came by revelation from God. The Lord Jesus Christ Himself announced that He would *build His church and the gates of hell shall not prevail against it.* (Matt.16:18).

According to the words of Jesus it was His intent to build a believer's church, a church that openly confesses Christ as the Son of God. When the Apostle Paul met with the elders from Ephesus he told them that God had purchased the church with His own blood.

> Acts 20:28; *Keep watch over yourselves and all the flock of which the Holy Spirit has made you overseers. Be shepherds of the church of God, which he bought with his own blood.*

Christ has been made head over all things to this blood-bought church.

> Eph 1:19-23...*and his incomparably great power for us who believe. That power is like the working of his mighty strength, which he exerted in Christ when he raised him from the dead and seated him at his right hand in the heavenly realms, far above all rule and authority, power and dominion, and every title that can be given, not only in the present age but also in the one to come. And God placed*

---

[13] ibid

*all things under his feet and appointed him to be head over everything for the church, which is his body, the fullness of him who fills everything in every way.*

From the biblical stand point the church is infinitely more than a social institution shaped by the culture. The leadership of the church is not free to introduce any innovation they may choose. As Paul wrote to Timothy,

1 Tim 3:15; *if I am delayed, you will know how people ought to conduct themselves in God's household, which is the church of the living God, the pillar and foundation of the truth.*

God's church here on Earth must not be shaped by the culture and the ever-changing social milieu that surrounds it. The church is the public manifestation of the saving grace of our Lord Jesus Christ. As such, Scripture has already prescribed the church's head, its doctrine, officers, worship, ordinances and message. When the church is truly abiding by the Scriptures, the church will be the instrument of God to positively change, shape, and influence every human culture and system of thought it touches. Most importantly, it brings to a people God's only plan of salvation, resulting in restored harmony with God.

## The Worshiping Church[14]

Since worship is the issue in this report, what does Scripture say about our worship? Music is an important aspect of true worship. Paul taught that the church was to be a singing church.

Eph 5:19; *Speak to one another with psalms, hymns and spiritual songs. Sing and make music in your heart to the Lord.*

Believers are to sing with the help of the Holy Spirit. The song may be in a language in any musical style consistent with psalms, hymns and spiritual songs. The songs must be sound in doctrine, pleasing to God and edifying to the believers. All worship must be done decently and in order.

1 Cor. 14:40 *But everything should be done in a fitting and orderly way.*

Some take the stand native churches should adapt from animistic practices ways of worship so the church will have a Native American identity. This supposition is based on the idea that native churches have been forced into a European model of worship. They go on to reason that a totally Native American format of worship must be developed to give the native church integrity. This argument does not hold up under

---

[14] ibid

careful scrutiny. Since true biblical worship is primarily done in Spirit and in truth, there will be common elements of worship evident in every culture in which it is engaged.

Across the entire history of Christianity, it has been crossing cultural lines. The first witnesses to the Gentile world were Jews with a very distinct culture. The first century church planted congregations among Greeks, Romans, Asians and Africans. The first council meeting of the church was to deal with the tensions with Gentiles over cultural issues (Acts 15). The problem was settled by the guidance of the Holy Spirit and the Word of God.

When the gospel was later preached in northern Europe and Britain the inhabitants of those countries were animists and upon conversion made a complete break with their old animistic worship. Much of their church worship and practice they inherited from those representatives of the church who brought them the gospel.

In many Anglo churches, Gregorian chants dating back centuries are still used in many churches. The hymns of the reformation period and revival periods of church history are sung with understanding in hundreds of languages all over the world.

Because of this reality in church history, the native Christian church has not been singled out on this issue. It is experiencing what every people group receiving the gospel has had to work through. It is part of the process of developing a truly indigenous church that is maintaining a healthy and biblical interdependence with the church at large.

The native church leadership must take the initiative in leading the native church through the process of receiving church worship and practice from outside our culture, as the starting point of developing true indigenous, biblically based worship. Each generation has the opportunity to contribute in this process, but sound biblical doctrine must be the defining principles that guide the church.

This does not mean there is no impact of culture on the worship in churches. The pattern has been the incorporation of western style hymnology in native churches, and where there has been true biblically based indigenous hymnology growing out of western style hymnology, it has been a rich blessing to the indigenous church, and occasionally even to the church at large. An example would be the beautiful *Hallelujah Song* of the Creeks and Seminoles, which has not only been sung in native churches, but was incorporated into the opening ceremonies of Promise Keeper's massive Stand in the Gap Sacred Assembly in Washington, D.C. in the fall of 1998.

This song is truly an indigenous hymn, and is clearly biblical, and was a tremendous blessing to the million plus men assembled on The Mall, and to a global television and radio audience.

The identifying characteristic of this and other similar Native American hymnology expressed in evangelical worship is its commitment to the guidelines of Scripture, while not reflecting animistic practices of the culture.

While it is true that native churches in the Americas sing Western hymns that they received from the missionaries, but in doing so, most tribes have put their own imprint on these hymns. One can visit native churches all across the Americas and would find that the style of worship is anything but a slavish imitation of Anglo worship. The preaching in native churches is most distinctive. The Western hymns are sung with a native flavor. The manner of conducting a service is often distinctly native.

Some native churches are content embracing western styles of hymnology. As long as western style hymnology does not conflict with biblical principles, and if the western style hymnology is meeting the needs of a particular native church, they should not feel obligated to move from western hymnology to a more indigenous hymnology. Western style hymnology, with their own unique native flavor, then, has become the indigenous form of worship for that church.

The Scriptures must be the wellspring of native worship just as they are in churches all over the world. A link must exist between the native congregations and the whole body of Christ in the Americas and the world. All Christians need the knowledge and experience of the larger church.

The unique cultural expressions of any people group should never overshadow the importance of each cultural group's relationship with the body of Christ at large.

## Demonology (Power Encounter)[15]

Since apostolic times the church has included demonology it its belief system. The Scriptures teach Satan and his demons are fallen angels. These powers of darkness oppose Christ and His church and attempt to deceive the church. Paul warns of the danger of the doctrines of demons in the last days.

1 Tim 4:1; *The Spirit clearly says that in later times some will abandon the faith and follow deceiving spirits and things taught by demons.*

The apostle John urged Christians to be cautious and test spiritual manifestations to determine if they are from God.

I Jn. 4:1-3; *Dear friends, do not believe every spirit, but test the spirits to see whether they are from God, because many false prophets have gone out into the world. This is how you can recognize the Spirit of God: Every spirit that acknowledges that Jesus Christ has come in the flesh is from God, but every spirit that does not acknowledge Jesus is not from God. This is the spirit of the antichrist, which you have heard is coming and even now is already in the world.*

---

[15] ibid

Beginning with the Old Testament God condemns animism. The actual practices of animism are named and declared to be an abomination to the Lord.

> Deut. 18:9-14; *When you enter the land the LORD your God is giving you, do not learn to imitate the detestable ways of the nations there. Let no one be found among you who sacrifices his son or daughter in the fire, who practices divination or sorcery, interprets omens, engages in witchcraft, or casts spells, or who is a medium or spiritist or who consults the dead. Anyone who does these things is detestable to the LORD, and because of these detestable practices the LORD your God will drive out those nations before you. You must be blameless before the LORD your God. The nations you will dispossess listen to those who practice sorcery or divination. But as for you, the LORD your God has not permitted you to do so.*

Satan is the intelligence and evil genius behind animism past and present. Israel was forbidden to dabble in animism. God Himself has drawn a line between His people and all animistic practices. Israel understood that to follow Jehovah God one must make a clean break with spirit worship in all its forms. It was their practice to destroy all the paraphernalia associated with the works of darkness.

2 Chr. 31:1; *When all this had ended, the Israelites who were there went out to the towns of Judah, smashed the sacred stones and cut down the Asherah poles. They destroyed the high places and the altars throughout Judah and Benjamin and in Ephraim and Manasseh. After they had destroyed all of them, the Israelites returned to their own towns and to their own property.*

II Ki. 18:4; *He removed the high places, smashed the sacred stones and cut down the Asherah poles. He broke into pieces the bronze snake Moses had made, for up to that time the Israelites had been burning incense to it.*

2 Chr. 34:33; *Josiah removed all the detestable idols from all the territory belonging to the Israelites, and he had all who were present in Israel serve the LORD their God. As long as he lived, they did not fail to follow the LORD, the God of their fathers.*

The items devoted to the spirits were destroyed because they were used to worship demons. The biblical principle of separation from all evil applies to this situation.

The New Testament takes the same stand as the Old Testament. God's people are warned against giving any place to the devil.

Eph. 4:27; *and do not give the devil a foothold.*

They are urged to renounce and resist the devil.

1 Pet. 5:8-9; *Be self-controlled and alert. Your enemy the devil prowls around like a roaring lion looking for someone to devour. Resist him, standing firm in the faith, because you know that your brothers throughout the world are undergoing the same kind of sufferings.*

James 4:7; *Submit yourselves, then, to God. Resist the devil, and he will flee from you.*

Animism as a demonic system invades the culture of any people that embrace it. When there are converts from animism they do not need to renounce their culture. They need only to renounce the evil infestation of spirit worship, which God hates. How the new believer sorts out culture is dictated by the principle of holiness God has implanted in their hearts. One can be a Christian and still be a true Native American. The Native American Christian on scriptural grounds draws a line when it comes to evil. He is willing to be counter-cultural in that which displeases the Lord in order to please the Lord. This would apply to any obedient believer in any culture.

The material artifacts (sacred objects) used by animists are never neutral, but dedicated to the demons. In most instances, they are actually indwelt by demons. There is not the faintest hint in the Bible that it is God's intention to redeem such objects. The idea of redeeming animistic objects comes from non-biblical sources.

The Scriptures are our final authority. All that the Bible has to say on this subject forbids the redeeming of the artifacts and practices of animism. The Christian is to destroy them and forever distance himself from the evil they represent.

### Doctrines of General Revelation and Special Revelation[16]

Among the papers and academic dissertations being circulated on the possibility of redeeming objects used in animistic worship, one finds an alarming trend to the new, *Wider Hope* theology. Simply put, this new teaching, which is invading evangelical circles suggests that animistic people may be sufficiently enlightened by general revelation to be saved. Misinterpreted biblical examples are cited to support this idea. This is the first step towards universalism.

So, what is the doctrine of General and Special Revelation?

### General Revelation

General Revelation is described in Paul's letter to the Romans.

Rom 1:18-21; *The wrath of God is being revealed from heaven against all the godlessness and wickedness of men*

---
[16] ibid

*who suppress the truth by their wickedness, since what may be known about God is plain to them, because God has made it plain to them. For since the creation of the world God's invisible qualities--his eternal power and divine nature-- have been clearly seen, being understood from what has been made, so that men are without excuse. For although they knew God, they neither glorified him as God nor gave thanks to him, but their thinking became futile and their foolish hearts were darkened.*

The natural creation makes known the God of creation. One can gaze on a beautiful mountain and understand that an intelligent and powerful God made this physical world.

Nothing Paul says in this passage suggests that the knowledge of this general revelation was sufficient to save. It only deepened their problem as Paul continued his thoughts to the Romans.

Rom 1:22-32; *Although they claimed to be wise, they became fools and exchanged the glory of the immortal God for images made to look like mortal man and birds and animals and reptiles. Therefore God gave them over in the sinful desires of their hearts to sexual impurity for the degrading of their bodies with one another. They exchanged the truth of God for a lie, and worshiped and served created things rather than the Creator-- who is forever praised. Amen. Because of this, God gave them over* to shameful lusts. Even their women exchanged natural relations for unnatural ones. In the same way the men also abandoned natural relations with women and were inflamed with lust for one another. Men committed indecent acts with other men, and received in themselves the due penalty for their perversion. Furthermore, since they did not think it worthwhile to retain the knowledge of God, he gave them over to a depraved mind, to do what ought not to be done. They have become filled with every kind of wickedness, evil, greed and depravity. They are full of envy, murder, strife, deceit and malice. They are gossips, slanderers, God-haters, insolent, arrogant and boastful; they invent ways of doing evil; they disobey their parents; they are senseless, faithless, heartless, ruthless. Although they know God's righteous decree that those who do such things deserve death, they not only continue to do these very things but also approve of those who practice them.

### Special Revelation

Special Revelation is the direct Word of God, revealed supernaturally to man. Adam and Eve were saved by special revelation, as God came to them and explained His provision for their forgiveness of sin. He added the wonderful promise of Christ, the coming Redeemer. Until the special revelation was written down, these revelations came directly from God to individuals.

Noah had special revelation from God on the Flood, and preached righteousness. Enoch had special revelation, and preached the Second Coming of Christ in the early years of human history. Abraham was saved through special revelation, as were all the patriarchs. The nation of Israel enjoyed special revelation at the mouths of their seers and prophets. Finally, special revelation was written and our complete Bible contains special revelation to those who live today. Special revelation is redemptive in nature. Men can only be saved through God's special revelation.

Some claim that animists could be saved through general revelation. They say that knowing the Creator God can effect salvation. Some proponents of the "redeeming the culture" movement propose that a native man dancing in a ritual of his animistic religion was worshiping the Creator. This teaching proposes worshiping the Creator apart from the person of Jesus Christ. The Bible says that Jesus Christ is the Creator.

> Heb 1:1-3; *In the past God spoke to our forefathers through the prophets at many times and in various ways, but in these last days he has spoken to us by his Son, whom he appointed heir of all things, and through whom he made the universe. The Son is the radiance of God's glory and the exact representation of his being, sustaining all things by his powerful word. After he had provided purification for sins, he sat down at the right hand of the Majesty in heaven.*

> John 1:1-3, 14, *In the beginning was the Word, and the Word was with God, and the Word was God. He was with God in the beginning. Through him all things were made; without him nothing was made that has been made. The Word became flesh and made his dwelling among us. We have seen his glory, the glory of the One and Only, who came from the Father, full of grace and truth.*

> Col 1:15-16; *He is the image of the invisible God, the firstborn over all creation. For by him all things were created: things in heaven and on earth, visible and invisible, whether thrones or powers or rulers or authorities; all things were created by him and for him.*

Worship not focused on Jesus, is not true worship of the Creator. This is overlooking and denying the doctrine of the Trinity as active in the work of creation. This constitutes false teaching and cannot be supported by biblical truth. As such, the apostle Paul in his letter to Timothy admonishes us,

> 2 Tim 4:1-4; *In the presence of God and of Christ Jesus, who will judge the living and the dead, and in view of his appearing and his kingdom, I give you this charge: Preach the Word; be prepared in season and out of season; correct, rebuke and encourage-- with great patience and careful instruction. For the time will come when men will not put up with sound doctrine. Instead, to suit their own desires,*

*they will gather around them a great number of teachers to say what their itching ears want to hear. They will turn their ears away from the truth and turn aside to myths.*

There is a subtle hint in some of their writings and teachings that animism is not as bad as we think. If they were able to prove that point, it would greatly strengthen their teaching that animistic practices can be redeemed. The difficulty with this theory is that it cannot be supported by any sound biblical hermeneutics.

Throughout Christian history, the belief that general revelation might save has dulled the missionary vision of the church. The idea that souls may be saved through general revelation opens the door to universalism. It promotes religious pluralism, characteristic of the liberal humanistic theologians. Salvation through the one true mediator, our Lord Jesus Christ, is the plain teaching of the Bible.

The only hope open to any sinner anywhere at any time and any place is Christ, the Way, the Truth, and the Life. The Gospel of Christ is special revelation. Salvation is by God, Himself. His instruction is to preach it to everybody in the entire world, because Christ is the Savior of the entire world.

*John 4:42; They said to the woman, "We no longer believe just because of what you said; now we have heard for ourselves, and we know that this man really is the Savior of the world."*

## Hermeneutics[17]

Hermeneutics is relevant to this Position Paper in that most advocates of redeeming culture appeal to Scripture for the support of their premise. It must be recognized that the interpretation of their proof texts reveal some of the new paradigms in the field of hermeneutics that have not been embraced by the Evangelical church at large.

F. F. Bruce writing in the Evangelical Dictionary of Theology gives a simple definition to hermeneutics,

> *A basic requirement for the understanding of these documents (meaning the Old and New Testaments) is their grammatico-historical interpretation or exegesis--bringing out of the text the meaning the writers intended to convey and which their readers were expected to gather from it.*[18]

The interpretation of Scripture calls for the consideration of the literary context of the passage, the historical background, geographical features, and the grammar of the text. F.F. Bruce sees hermeneutics as giving the church God's Word in its primary sense and meaning.

The existential hermeneutic asks the Bible student to place himself in a position so as to experience what the writer might be saying. This form of hermeneutics rests on a philosophical

---

[17] ibid

[18] ibid

supposition that only what is presently experienced is real. Such a system of interpretation by its very nature denies the concept of absolute truth. Relativism is a primary feature of this style of hermeneutics.

Since we believe that the original manuscript of the Bible is the inerrant, infallible, inspired Word of God, valid interpretation must rest on the grammatico-historical approach to hermeneutics.

In the contemporary scene, the Bible and culture has become a major concern. Hermeneutics is a key player in this arena. It should be recognized up front that the secular educational disciplines of anthropology and sociology have influenced how many think about the interpretation of Scripture. There is a school of missiologists who have built a theology of culture on extra-biblical sources. These same scholars have accepted the secular view of relativism.

Charles Kraft, from Fuller Seminary, goes so far as to say,

*God takes into account the relativity of the human situation and that human accountability is relative to the extent of revelational material received. God adjusts his expectations to the cultural patterns of each society.*

Kraft's position is unacceptable to those who accept the authority of Scripture. As a result of the new cultural hermeneutic, numerous writers favoring the "redemption of culture", quote 2 Corinthians 5:17 as a proof text. This verse says,

*Therefore, if anyone is in Christ, the new creation has come: The old has gone, the new is here!*

Applying a culture and a community based hermeneutic to interpret the passage, they then can suggest that the expression "the new is here, " supports the idea that the old animistic ways can be redeemed. The only problem with this interpretation is that it completely ignores the context of the passage. It overlooks the plain sense of the verse, which says that regeneration of an individual (not cultural forms) is a total spiritual transformation in the life of one who believes on Christ.

The expression, "The old has gone," if using a grammatico-historical hermeneutic, declares the removal of the old behavior of the sinner replacing it with the new life in Christ for the redeemed one. There is no ground for the redemption of culture in this passage. It refers only to the change brought about by Christ in the personal life of an individual.[19]

As I once again reviewed the content of *Boundary Lines,* I was grateful for being a part of the process that helped our indigenous churches in The C&MA (US) know the difference between truth and error. We've been the better for it. As our churches stand today on these theological positions, my hope and prayer is that you, too, will better understand what God's

---

[19] *Boundary Lines, The Issue of Christ, Indigenous Worship and Native American Culture.* The Native American Association of The Christian and Missionary Alliance (US).

Word has to say on these matters, and how to detect for yourself truth from error.

While teaching on these important issues I am constantly reminded about the strong battle we are in for truth. I am saddened by how many good men and women, leaders in the North American indigenous church, are being led astray from biblical truth by embracing a *what I think* theology. I would warn us with great passion about the danger of this *what I think* theology.

Case in point...

I recently was teaching *Indigenous Faith* to a group of Native and non-Native ministry leaders. As I was promoting a return to the authority of Scripture, several missionaries and the Native people they led, got up and walked out.

At another recent conference, a Native pastor stood up and debated me about the biblical position on redeeming sacred objects. His whole argument rested on what he *thought* about the issue. He noted, *I do not consider these things sacred to me, so I can redeem them and use them.* He made this statement just after I had taken about an hour to unpackage from Scripture what God had to say about redeeming sacred objects. What seemed to matter most to him, in my opinion, was what his thoughts were on the issue, regardless of what the Scriptures had to say.

There is great danger in believing our thoughts or convictions have greater authority than the revealed Word of God. In all honesty, it really doesn't matter what he or even

I think. The bottom line is, what does God think about these matters? Thankfully, we have His revealed Word to know and understand. That's why syncretists building theological positions on non-biblical thought are on very dangerous ground. A *what I think* theology is built not just on sand, but on sinking sand.

It is going to be important to keep these theological concepts in mind as we journey together through the remainder of this book. The beautiful scenes we will visit from God's Word will be the highlights of this trip down the biblical road of truth.

## Chapter Four

# WHOSE TRUTH IS TRUTH?

IF YOU WERE TO ASK THOSE IN THE KNOW IN THE OVER five-hundred-sixty some federally recognized Native American tribes, *What is your traditional story of origin*, you'd no doubt hear some interesting yet different responses to that question. Take for example what is told by Mr. Eddie Benton Benai, an educator and traditional *Midewiwin* religious leader from Wisconsin, about our Ojibwe story of origin.

> *Boo-zhoo' (hello), my name is Mishomis. I am an Ojibwe Indian. I would like to tell you an account of how man was created on this Earth. This teaching was handed down by word of mouth from generation to generation by my ancestors. Sometimes the details of teachings like this were recorded on scrolls made from Wee'-gwas (birch bark). I am fortunate to be the keeper of several of these scrolls. They will help me remember some of the details of what I give to you.*

*Indigenous Faith*

When Ah-ki' (the Earth) was young, it was said that the Earth had a family. Nee-ba-gee'-sis (the Moon) is called Grandmother, and Gee'-sis (the Sun) is called Grandfather. The Creator of this family is called Gi'-tchie Man-i-to' (Great Mystery or Creator). The Earth is said to be a woman. In this way it is understood that woman preceded man on the Earth. She is called Mother Earth because from her come all living things. Water is her life's blood. It flows through her, nourishes her, and purifies her.

On the surface of the Earth, all is given Four Sacred Directions--North, South, East, and West. Each of these directions contributes a vital part to the wholeness of the Earth. Each has physical powers as well as spiritual powers, as do all things. When she was young, the Earth was filled with beauty. The Creator sent his singers in the form of birds to the Earth to carry the seeds of life to all of the Four Directions. In this way life was spread across the Earth. On the Earth the Creator placed the swimming creatures of the water. He gave life to all the plant and insect world. He placed the crawling things and the four-leggeds on the land. All of these parts of life lived in harmony with each other. Gitchie Manito then took four parts of Mother Earth and blew into them using a Sacred Shell. From the union of the Four Sacred Elements and his breath, man was created. It is said the Gitchie Manito then lowered man to the Earth. Thus, man was the last form of life to be placed on Earth. From this Original Man came the A-nish-i-na'-be people. In the Ojibwe language if you break down the word Anishinabe, this is what it means: ANI (from whence) NISHINA (lowered) ABE (the male of the species). This man was created in the image of Gitchie Manito. He was natural man. He was part of Mother Earth. He lived in brotherhood with all that was around him. All tribes came from this Original Man. The Ojibwe are a tribe because of the way they speak. We believe that we are nee-kon'-nis-ug' (brothers) with all tribes; we are separated only by our tongue or language.

Today, the Ojibwes cherish the Megis Shell as the Sacred Shell through which the Creator blew his breath. The Megis was to appear and reappear to the Ojibwe throughout their history to show them the Path that the Creator wished them to follow. Some Ojibwe Indians today wear the Megis or Cowrie shell to remember the origin of man and the history of their people.

There are a few people in each of the tribes that have survived to this day who have kept alive their teachings, language, and religious ceremonies. Although traditions may differ from tribe to tribe, there is a common thread that runs throughout them all. This common thread represents a string of lives that goes back all the way to Original Man. Today, we need to use this kinship of all Indian people to give us the strength necessary to keep our traditions alive. No one way is better than another.

> *I have heard my grandfathers say that there are many roads to the High Place. We need to support each other by respecting and honoring the "many roads" of all tribes. The teachings of one tribe will shed light on those of another. It is important that we know our native language, our teachings, and our ceremonies so that we will be able to pass this sacred way of living on to our children and continue the string of lives of which we are a living part. Mi-gwetch' (thank-you)!*[20]

Compare this account with what my wife's tribe, the Navajo, have to say about how life began.

> *First man and first woman were created by the Holy People (basketmakers), and brought to the surface through a series of underworlds. The Navajo story of their origin is long and complicated with many versions varying to as having come through twelve underworlds grouped by fours into three layers, or "rooms" which are also called worlds. We will find this story. And we did. Here is a short version:*
>
> *Only the Creator knows where the beginning is. The Creator had a thought that created Light in the East. Then the thought went South to create Water, West to create Air, and North to create Pollen from emptiness. This Pollen became Earth. Light, air, water, and Earth is contained in*

---

[20] Excerpt taken from *The Mishomish Book,* Eddie Benton Benai, 1988

*everything within nature; all of the natural world is interconnected and equal.*

*All of these elements mixed together, and the first thing created were the Holy People. These Holy People were given the job and responsibility of teaching what is right and wrong. Holy people were given the original laws, then they created the Earth and human beings.*

*The Creator with the help of the Holy People created the Natural World. They created humans, birds, and all of the Natural World was put in Hozjo (BALANCE). This Hozjo (harmony, balance, and peace) is dependent on interconnectedness. All of the Natural World depends on another. The Navajo say they are glued together with respect, and together they work in harmony. To the Navajo this present world is the fifth.*

*The place of emergence into this level was Xajiinai, a hole in the La Plata mountains of SW Colorado. The Holy People have the power to hurt or help, and centuries ago taught the Dineh (Navajo) how to live in harmony with Mother Earth, Father Sky and the other elements: man, animals, plants, insects. The Dineh believe that when the ceremonies cease the world will cease.*[21]

Circle the globe and ask other indigenous peoples their story of origins, and you will continue to find divergent

---

[21] http://www.ausbcomp.com/redman/navajo.htm

recitations of traditions, histories, and stories that stand in stark contrast one from the other.

Now I do not mean to disparage any tribe, group, or people, but the obvious question is, who is right? *Whose truth is truth?*

You've got two different accounts of how mankind got here not to mention the dirt on which we all stand. Is one account right thus making the other one wrong? Do the Navajos understand something that we Ojibwe do not, or is it easier to accept, as Mr. Benton Benai states, *there are many roads to the High Place. We need to support each other by respecting and honoring the "many roads" of all tribes.*

Universalism has found its place in indigenous theology and tradition.

For the Christian, there is only one place you can go to find truth. In a world of divergent thought, God's Word stands out as universal truth that gives us a window into the mind and heart of the One who made the universe. Within its pages is doctrinal truth about the Creator Himself and all He created. For the Christian, it provides the sole source of the beauty of the Creation story, original man, original sin, and God's redemption plan that was laid out according to the Scriptures, beginning in Genesis 1:1.

## The Creator According to the Scriptures

Travel across indigenous country today, and you'd be hard pressed to find indigenous people who hold to an atheistic belief system. We aren't atheists, but largely hold to a worldview that acknowledges the existence of the spirit world, the supernatural, and the affirmation of a creator of it all. But is the creator in indigenous traditional belief systems the same as the Creator of the Bible? What does the Word of God have to say about our Maker?

The Bible offers a clear and compelling case of a triune God, with three distinct persons, yet these three are One.

Only an infinite God can adequately explain Himself, and yet we try to do so with such feeble efforts through the foggy lens of our finiteness. That is why we're on much firmer ground when we simply rest on the authority of the revealed Scriptures, God's Holy Word!

Scripture clearly identifies all parts of the Trinity as active in the original creation of the universe, including this earth and all the animate and inanimate objects that inhabit it. Three verses (among others) come to mind that clearly identify the Father, Son, and Holy Spirit as active in the works of creation.

Here's the Father:
*Yet you, Lord, are our Father. We are the clay, you are the potter; we are all the work of your hand. (Isaiah 64:8)*

Here's the Son:
*The Son is the image of the invisible God, the firstborn over all creation. For in him all things were created: things in heaven and on Earth, visible and invisible, whether thrones or powers or rulers or authorities; all things have been created through him and for him. He is before all things, and in him all things hold together. (Colossians 1:15–17)*

Here's the Holy Spirit:
*The Spirit of God has made me; the breath of the Almighty gives me life. (Job 33:4)*

While all three parts of the Trinity are responsible for creation, God in His sovereign inspiration of Scripture chooses to single out the Son, Jesus the Christ, for particular honor and mention as not only the *agent*, but the very *reason* for the existence of all created things.

In John's gospel we read;

*In the beginning was the Word (Christ Jesus), and the Word was with God, and the Word was God. He was with God in the beginning. Through him all things were made;*

*without him nothing was made that has been made. (John 1:1-3).*

As we just saw in Colossians, Paul further explains;

*The Son (Christ Jesus) is the image of the invisible God, the firstborn over all creation. For in him all things were created: things in heaven and on earth, visible and invisible, whether thrones or powers or rulers or authorities; all things have been created through him and for him. (Colossians 1:15-16).*

The writer of Hebrews reiterates once again Christ as the Creator as clearly and compellingly as possible when he states;

*In the past God spoke to our ancestors through the prophets at many times and in various ways, but in these last days he has spoken to us by his Son (Christ Jesus), whom he appointed heir of all things, and through whom also he made the universe. (Hebrews 1:1-2).*[22]

It is abundantly clear that the biblical Creator was none other than Jesus Christ, the God who became the God-man, who walked on Planet Earth some two thousand years ago!

---

[22] parenthetical inserts added for clarification in all three passages.

Why is the singling out of the Son in creation so important to an infinite God as He reveals Himself to his finite creation through His Word?

I believe it is so because this Creator came down and became part of His creation when God the Son put on human feet, legs, arms, body, and head, and those feet touched Planet Earth. God the Son is the One who so closely identifies with the creation He created, yet remains outside the belief systems of indigenous theologies which do not acknowledge Christ as Creator.

Throughout history, the world has been perfectly fine to speak generically about "God and creator" as many cultures do. Bring in the name of Jesus, however, and you'll have angry sparks of protest and denial by many who cannot stand the thought of Christ as Divine and as the *sole agent* and *reason* for all that has been created.

Creation actually touched and felt Divinity. Mary nursed the very One who created her. Joseph actually trained heaven and earth's Creator in the skills of a carpenter, and baby John, while yet in his mother womb, leapt for joy when Jesus, still being carried about in Mary's womb, entered the same room!

The Creator of the Bible is the Creator of the universe, and there is non-other who comes within a thousand universes of this awesome God who made it all!

I say this with all due respect to my people, and to people groups worldwide, whose faith is genuine and sincere as aligned with traditional indigenous theologies. But say it I must! Based on the revealed Word of God, God the Father, God the Son, and God the Holy Spirit - the God of the revealed Scriptures, is the One and Only Creator of heaven and earth! That's not because I say it, but because the universal truth of God's Holy Word says it!

Biblically aligned *Indigenous Faith* must affirm Christ as Creator. This truth anchors all other aspects of our faith if we are to *live out a biblically healthy life in the context of an Indigenous culture.*

I say so with great passion and a deep burden in my heart. We are missing the real thing for a replacement creator, to whom the enemy of the souls of a thousand people groups desires we cling to, worship, and celebrate.

Why? Because Satan is fine with us having religion, any religion, as long as it is not based on Jesus Christ! Turn from indigenous theological tradition to faith in Jesus Christ, and you will see Satan's anger and hostility turn toward you. Even as I write this, many Christ followers from cultures around the world are having their heads cut off by radicals promoting religions contrary to God's Holy Word.

Ask the nations if their traditional religious dogmas embrace or identify Jesus Christ as the Creator they worship. The answer will without question be absolutely not! It is possible to be a creationist while rejecting the very Creator who made all things.

As the pages of this book unfold, the Creator I am speaking of is the true Creator of heaven and earth, Jesus the Christ – the Christ of Christianity, the Christ of the revealed Word of God!

This is a critical point I need to make here, my friend. Because the promoters of the *Redeeming the Culture* movement have some key presuppositions that guide their thinking. One of those is that Creator God, as a part of His creative genius, gave to all the nations of the world their own unique and distinctive cultural ways and spiritualities. Because of that, all those ways receive His sanction and blessing.

The question is, my friend, where in Scripture do you find that happening? Can you take me to the chapter and verses that tell us God gave each and every nation their distinct cultures and spiritualities?

But before you can answer that question, there's another question that helps us understand whether or not Scripture is even that important in these matters. It is another extremely important question because it identifies the real core issue at stake in all this confusion. The largest issue this movement raises is not the issue of proper cultural contextualization, but the issue of *the authority of Scripture itself*!

## What is our View of Scripture?

For over four decades I've been a licensed minister with The Christian and Missionary Alliance (C&MA). It is a well-respected evangelical family of churches and missionaries who are committed to taking the gospel of Jesus Christ to the ends of the earth.

Founded by Dr. A.B. Simpson in 1887, many faithful people have served in Alliance ministries around the globe. The lives and deaths of Alliance missionary martyrs have paved the way for national churches to be established in countries near and far. Thousands of servants of Christ have been privileged to carry C&MA credentials, myself included.

One thing we all have in common is a commitment to The C&MA's *Statement of Faith* which guides and governs our theological thought and convictions. The Statement covers a wide variety of theological issues including our position and understanding of Scripture. It is found in Article 4, where it states;

> *The Old and New Testaments, inerrant as originally given, were verbally inspired by God and are a complete revelation of His will for the salvation of men. They constitute the divine and only rule of Christian faith and practice.*[23]

---

[23] http://www.cmalliance.org/about/beliefs/doctrine

This Statement affirms our belief in the inerrancy, inspiration, and sufficiency of Scripture to guide us in all things pertaining to Christian faith and practice. The C&MA stands unapologetically committed to a *high view* of Scripture.

Having this view affirms the authority of Scripture in the life of the believer. But there is a danger in it when Scripture is processed intellectually alone and not through the guidance of the Holy Spirit.

Well known and oft times quoted Alliance leader, Dr. A.W. Tozer, refers to this as the error of *textualism*. This is maintaining an intellectual affirmation of the Scriptural text, while denying the vital work of the Holy Spirit in bringing enlightenment of these truths to the reader. He notes;

> *Fundamentalism has stood aloof from the Liberal in self-conscious superiority and has on its own part fallen into error, the error of textualism, which is simply orthodoxy without the Holy Ghost. Everywhere among Conservatives we find persons who are Bible-taught but not Spirit-taught. They conceive truth to be something which they can grasp with the mind. If a man holds to the fundamentals of the Christian faith he is thought to possess divine truth. But it does not follow. There is no truth apart from the Spirit. The most brilliant intellect may be imbecilic when confronted with the mysteries of God. For a man to understand revealed truth requires an act of God equal to the original act which inspired the text.*

> Conservative Christians in this day are stumbling over this truth. We need to re-examine the whole thing. We need to learn that truth consists not in correct doctrine, but in correct doctrine plus the inward enlightenment of the Holy Spirit. We must declare again the mystery of wisdom from above. A re-preachment of this vital truth could result in a fresh breath from God upon a stale and suffocating orthodoxy.[24]

From my experience crossing cultures all my life, the danger of *textualism* is especially evident with believers and even leaders in the Body of Christ who have been raised in Western Civilization and cultures. By and large, Western thought denies the existence of the supernatural realm. When a person comes to faith in Christ, he or she must now embrace the very existence of a supernatural God and the supernatural world He created. This is totally in contrast to their pre-Christian upbringing. It is not an easy transition. I urge my brothers and sisters in Christ, and especially leaders within our movements to understand, as Dr. Tozer notes, the importance of both Spirit and truth in our lives.

A high view of Scripture is not the only way Christians and denominations view God's Word, unfortunately. There are some who claim to be in the Christian camp but maintain what is referred to as a *low view* of Scripture.

---

[24] A. W. Tozer, The Pursuit of Man, 76-77,84.

These folks are easily identifiable by their beliefs that Scripture is not without error and not the complete revelation of God to man. They go to sources other than the Scriptures to guide and influence them on matters of theological importance. In this camp, Scripture is subject to the interpretation of the day. It is based on other than biblical sources such as culture and current intellectual thought. Misapplied Scripture is but one of many tools in the toolkit of compromisers and false teachers. The lack of the enlightenment of the Holy Spirit is brutally evident in employing this position, so it involves embracing of neither Spirit nor truth.

Making a biblical case for theological positions isn't all that important to this camp. But I truly believe it does! How we process theological matters through the searchlight of Scripture is incredibly important. I can choose to believe certain points on matters of importance if I like. However, if my convictions have been established on something other than biblical truth, it is quite possible I am building a belief system that, at its core, is based on something less than the truth, or no truth at all.

When one has a high view of Scripture you allow your theological convictions to be shaped by the Word of God alone. When doing so, you are standing on a solid foundation of that God given *faith, once and for all delivered to the saints.*

So, what does the Bible have to say about humanity, culture, nations, and how we all got to where we are today? Believe me, there's enough revealed truth in Scripture on these matters to give us everything we need to know from the *divine and only rule of Christian faith and practice,* God's Holy Word!

*Chapter Five*

# NO OTHER OPTION

---

ALONG WITH THE IMPORTANCE OF MAINTAINING A HIGH view of Scripture comes a clear and compelling call to not be ambivalent about protecting its truths and defending the faith, even if it means going against the cultural tides that move so much of false teaching along.

Ministry among North America's indigenous people can only be described as historically challenging and difficult for the missionary groups that have chosen to take up the call. At times, however, it has also been hard on the people groups that the gospel was intending to reach. The awkwardness of the larger history of relationships between Native American people and the immigrants who have come to this *New World* has produced less than good fertile soil for the planting of the seeds of the gospel. This has resulted in a less than abundant harvest.

Some indigenous people I know would argue, from their Native perspective, that Christianity is the great enemy of the soul of tribal people. Why? Because of both perceived and real experiences that built hostility between the two people groups. All too often a misrepresented Christianity was at the center of those experiences.

It is important to note, however, that the popular position of blaming the White man and White supremacy for all our problems fails to recognize an important reality. Long before the White man ever came to our shores, our indigenous tribes were committing similar atrocities against each other. An honest historical overview of North American history cannot ignore this painful fact.

All cultures play from the same playbook of common and fallen humanity. Without hesitation, this blindness tends to make us comfortable in pointing out the savagery of other cultures, while at the same time, conveniently overlooking horrific acts that were manifested by our own people.

It is clear that both positive and negative things were done between the new and the old inhabitants of this land in the five hundred plus years of the great American and Canadian experiments. Christianity's representatives have played their parts in the totality of the unfolding dramas of our national histories.

In many cases the cross-cultural missionaries that came to live among our tribal people have had very positive influences. Many even held places of honor and respect within the tribes and for that I celebrate!

Their investment in communities far and wide have brought hope and healing to many bodies, souls, and spirits.

They helped preserve languages that were being lost and stood up for the folks in less than fair courtrooms and legal proceedings. This resulted in the same level of goodwill that tribes showed to their own revered elders and leaders.

I do not think I'd be here today, as a committed follower of Jesus Christ, if it hadn't been for God empowering and using faithful C&MA missionaries. Their impact has made an incredible difference for the good in my family, now down to the fifth generation!

They got it right as they faithfully fulfilled the Great Commission's mandate of making disciples among the nations. Their impact continues to shape our family and will be felt in generations to come. It is a great story and has led me to embrace as my life's verse - Psalms 102:18;

*Let this be written for a future generation, that a people not yet created may praise the Lord.*

Conversely, history points to some who came representing Christ but ended up committing unimaginable acts of violence and abuse. This happened among the most vulnerable aboriginal people, especially the children. It happened primarily through programs and efforts embedded in government funded and church run residential boarding schools, such as the ones you would find in Canada's recent history.

It has led to a recent reconciliation movement between First Nations people, the Canadian government, and a wide variety of church denominations who were primary administrators of these institutions. The end goal has been to offer help to generations who have been deeply scarred through atrocities too painful to even describe.

It was never so poignant to me than a few years ago while meeting with ministry leaders in northwest Ontario while planning evangelism outreaches in their communities.

We were meeting in a hotel conference room at 7:00 p.m., where I was to present a ministry opportunity that would reach out to Native youth through the On Eagles' Wings® Native youth team, which I was directing at the time.[25] We were hoping to bring the team into the region that summer, reaching out to hurting indigenous youth, many of whom came from Native communities where hope is hard to come by.

While waiting for the event to start, I was reading the local newspaper and was drawn to a very unique advertisement found tucked away in the corner of one of the back pages. The headline read, *For the Survivors of the Christian Faith*. It was promoting a meeting at 7:00 p.m., exactly one week from the meeting I was hosting in this very same conference room.

The ad was encouraging aboriginal people who suffered abuse in the church run Residential School system. They

---

[25] A native youth ministry of Ron Hutchcraft Ministries, Inc., Harrison, AR.

were being asked to share their stories of survival, learn about the legal liability, and settlement arrangements being negotiated for those responsible for the atrocities spanning over a 125-year period.

I couldn't get that image out of my mind as I met that night with a room full of pastors and missionaries who were finding themselves having to minister today under the shadow of such history and deep pain. It makes ministry among our indigenous people in North America much more challenging.

It also provides fertile ground for less than biblical teaching to push its way into the Body of Christ. The Christianity being offered by the *Redeeming of Culture* movement is one that fits more with the narrative that elevates human culture and traditions over Scripture.

In this day and age, Scripture has been devalued. Transcendent truth is no longer relevant. Universal principles of holiness and godliness, as originally giving by inspiration of God, matter little any more.

We need to see beyond the rhetoric that the mutual enemy of our souls, in the Crayola Box of humanity, is promoting in the aftermath of historical trauma. This kind of trauma, done by those claiming to be representatives of Christ, never was or ever will be, sanctioned by the very God they claimed to represent. Be assured, the God of all the universe and the Judge of all things will not let such atrocities go unpunished by His Almighty hand.

We must never, as the Body of Christ, succumb to the enemy's plan to render the true saving gospel of Jesus Christ as impotent in today's present cultural realities as difficult as they may seem. Despite the fact our predecessors in Christian ministry at times did do wrong, Christ's Commission in Acts 1:8 is still in effect and must be obeyed until completed. What we must do is learn from these mistakes and ensure they are never repeated again.

To my indigenous brothers and sisters who use these historical atrocities to give you reason to reject Christ, I'd ask you to consider the truth that Jesus never said, *Follow my followers!* He said, *Follow Me!*

With all sincerity, if you are going to reject Christ, what issue do you have with Him? If you are going to reject the gospel message because of the flaws of human messengers, it will have eternal consequences. Every human being will stand before the God of the Bible and give an account for what they did with Christ. He's not going to ask you, *Why didn't you follow My followers?* Make no mistake, He will ask you, *Why didn't you follow Me?*

What brings comfort to my broken heart over these painful atrocities is the words of Abraham as recorded in Genesis 18:25.

He prayerfully and rhetorically states;

*Will not the Judge of all the earth do right?*

If I can offer any comfort to anyone who has suffered at the hands of an abuser, it is these comforting words. Full justice in this life is oft times elusive. We do ourselves additional grief and pain if we hope to find it in this life alone.

That doesn't mean we shouldn't pursue justice here on earth. That is an important part of the process, but so often we are disappointed by the outcomes when human judges and juries render decisions that do not give us the justice we seek. We then suffer a second round of abuse. How painful is that?

In all fairness, please remember that He does have to judge all people, including you and me, just as much as those that you may have deep resentment, bitterness, or hatred towards. God's judgement is both fair and comprehensive. 2 Corinthians 5:10 reminds us;

*For we must all appear before the judgment seat of Christ, so that each of us may receive what is due us for the things done while in the body, whether good or bad.*

Every thought, word, and deed that is accumulated on your and my accounts in heaven's record will be laid bare before our Creator. In the midst of your personal pain and anger at others, are you prepared to account for every deed done in your lifetime? It is true that for all of us, nothing has escaped the gaze and memory of an all-powerful, all knowing God!

The real answer to the hurt in your soul will never be found in a pursuit of culture or tradition, or reconciliation on merely a human level. It can only be found through the saving work of Jesus Christ. The Scriptures says it best when it quotes Jesus in John 10:10;

*I have come that they may have life, and have it to the full.*

I can assure you from my own life journey, I have found Jesus Christ to be the only One powerful enough to help me overcome painful abuse suffered in my own life.

He enabled me to forgive one of our own tribal men who kidnapped me at the age of five and threatened my life. After laying my head on the railroad tracks just behind our home he told me that if I didn't do what he said, he would let the train run me over and it would cut off my head. After hours in his clutches and suffering very painful abuse, I was eventually found by the police and returned safely to our home. That was back in the day when these kinds of events were addressed with much less justice and punishment than what our present-day system provides.

That is a whole lot to overcome, but overcome it I did! My victory came from my faith and trust in Jesus Christ, who also suffered abuse that took him through death's door on my behalf. I believed what Jesus taught me in His Word. He also gave me the power to forgive and not be chained to unforgiveness that would rob me from embracing life and living it to its fullest here on earth!

Because of Jesus and His power, I do not live in my own self-imposed prison of anger, frustration, and dysfunctional behavior. Through Christ, I've released my perpetrator into the hands of *the Judge of all the earth who will do right*! That makes me a free man now. I am not bound and handicapped by the actions of another who chose to do me harm. That's the kind of freedom Christ offers, my friend! That's the freedom He died to give us!

I also want to reiterate this admonition to the Body of Christ to emphasize this critically important point. We, too, must move forward in the power of the Holy Spirit, and not compromise or succumb to the awkwardness of past misdeeds of predecessors who did wrong. We must keep on preaching the gospel because that is the only message given to us whereby men and women can be saved, which includes being forgiven, healed, and transformed! That's the total package of the incredible gospel message!

One of the primary roles the New Testament profiles for church leaders is to do two critically important things. First, we are called to promote sound teaching and secondly, to refute and stand against false teaching. The issues described above must never give permission for the body of Christ and its leaders to jettison our responsibility in these important matters.

Scripture admonishes the Body of Christ in very clear language:

*You must teach what is in accord with sound doctrine (Titus 2:1).*

*Remember the words that were spoken beforehand by the apostles of our Lord Jesus Christ (Jude 1:17).*

Regardless of the cultural circumstances we find ourselves ministering in, we have no choice but to guard our congregations from doctrine not found in God's Word.

*Holding fast the faithful word as he has been taught, that he may be able, by sound doctrine, both to exhort and convict those who contradict. (Titus 1:9).*

*For the time will come when they will not endure sound doctrine, but according to their own desires, because they have itching ears, they will heap up for themselves teachers; and they will turn their ears away from the truth, and be turned aside to fables. But you be watchful in all things, endure afflictions, do the work of an evangelist, fulfill your ministry (2 Timothy 4:3-5).*

Throughout church history false teaching has always followed the gospel and its messengers around. It seeks to

# Indigenous Faith

confuse people and deflect revealed truth with error that can easily go undetected by followers of Christ who aren't avid students of God's Word.

If Satan can't stop the spread of the gospel, his next ploy will always be to stop the influence of the gospel by causing believers in Christ to follow other than biblical truth. The kind of Christianity offered by syncretistic teaching isn't something new to the church at large, but up to recently has been rejected by evangelicalism. But that is changing rapidly.

This movement's historical roots have been found within Catholicism and among more liberal Protestant churches, because they do not embrace a high view of Scripture.

Catholicism, in its less than stellar commitment to the authority of Scripture, has long elevated and promoted the church as primary over the Scriptures. Its leaders, including the varied popes who have served over its history, offer edicts and doctrine that are understood to be co-equal with that of the revealed Scriptures. *Papal infallibility also belongs to the body of bishops as a whole, when, in doctrinal unity with the pope, they solemnly teach a doctrine as true.*[26]

The selling of indulgences (the permitting of sin by the laity and escaping of its consequences by financial payments to the Church's clergy) by the Catholic Church half a millennium ago was rampant. It caused one of its own priests, Martin Luther, to protest the church's horrific deviations from the biblical truth of historic Christianity. It led

---

[26] https://www.catholic.com/tract/papal-infallibility

him to post his Ninety-Five Thesis on the door of Wittenberg Church on October 31, 1517, challenging the Catholic Church on its position on indulgences and other important theological issues. It led to the Protestant Reformation, ultimately dividing Christianity into two key church groups, the Catholics and the Protestants.

Over time liberal Protestantism became just as guilty of denying the authority of the Scriptures as its Catholic counterparts. That's why in both their North American indigenous churches today you'll see a blending of Christianity with Native traditional spiritual practices. In modern indigenous Catholic and liberal Protestant churches, you can find syncretistic worship on full display. Along with the rites, Mass, and liturgical services, you will often find the incorporation of sweat lodge ceremonies, the smells of the tobacco, sage, and sweet grass filling the sanctuary, as smudging ceremonies are performed as a more *cultural expression* of Christian faith and practice.

The syncretism pushing its way into modern evangelicalism flows not only historically from Catholicism and liberal Protestantism but more recently through the modern independent Charismatic movement.

Within this part of the Body of Christ, the *Rhema* (continual spoken) word from God stands with equal authority and relevance alongside the *Logos* (written) Word of God.

It is not my intent, in this book, to debate the issues that divided the *Rhema* camp from the *Logos* camp within modern Protestant evangelical Christianity. I only seek to provide as much information here that helps us understand how this movement has found its way into, and is sustaining itself within, the modern Native evangelical ministry scene.

The *Rhema* of God gives room for God to continue to speak to His church today through not only the revealed Scriptures but through a contemporary human voice as well. I am not talking about the preaching and the teaching of God's Word, but of spontaneous prophetic and extra-biblical utterances common within the Charismatic movement.

*Thus saith the Lord*, is often the precursor statement that introduces what the speaker contemporaneously says is the *new word from the Lord*.

The question is, how do you know that your *Rhema* word is truly from God? 1 Timothy 4:1 gives caution to all as the Apostle Paul states;

> *The Spirit clearly says that in later times some will abandon the faith and follow deceiving spirits and things taught by demons.*

Some of the leaders of the current *Redeeming of Culture* movement have been spiritually raised in the modern Charismatic movement. They have stated unequivocally their convictions that God has given them His blessing and favor to promote this form of teaching.

Their *all in* embracing of this doctrine has led to a passionate proclaiming and following of this new revelation, including the redeeming of sacred objects formerly used in animistic worship. In their mind, and even occasionally articulated, they deemed that this *special enlightenment* came to them from God through prophetic *Rhema* revelations.

My heartfelt admonition is this. Take a lesson from the Gnostics of the past, who believed they had a special and unique revelation from God, which set them apart from the rest of the Christians in the infant days of the New Testament Church. The problem was, their special revelation was no revelation at all. Their teaching stood in stark contrast with what the New Testament writers were teaching and articulating in their letters to the churches. As we know, these epistles eventually established true New Testament doctrine.

As an example (and there are many more), the Gnostics held to the following theological position about who Christ was;

> *As far as most scholars know, Gnostics considered themselves Christians and saw Jesus as a heavenly messenger. However, they rejected the idea of God becoming incarnate (God becoming a man), dying and rising bodily. "These beliefs were considered unspiritual and against true wisdom because they entangled spirit with matter."*

*Most Gnostics believe that whoever entered Jesus at his baptism left him before he died on the cross.[27]*

In evaluating this current *Redeeming of Culture* movement, it led a dear Mohawk friend of mine, and Native denominational leader within the Assemblies of God (US), Rev. John Maracle, to describe this movement as simply *new Gnosticism.*

If I could span the two camps for a moment, I'd plead the following. *If you have a fresh new Rhema word from God, then at minimum, please, evaluate whether or not that Rhema word aligns itself clearly with the already revealed Logos of God!*

The real challenge is, my friend, your word has to be measured against His Word, and if your word doesn't align with His once and for all Word, I am going to go with His Word every time! The importance of the very last verse in Scripture is what every assumed *Rhema* word of God will be measured against. For it says in Revelation 22:18,

*I warn everyone who hears the words of the prophecy of this scroll: If anyone adds anything to them, God will add to that person the plagues described in this scroll.*

An important admonition my friend!

---

[27] The Story of Christian Theology, p. 37

# PART 2
# DISCOVERING THE TRUTH

*Chapter Six*

# THE BIBLICAL ANATOMY OF CULTURE

TODAY'S *REDEEMING OF CULTURE* MOVEMENT IS PRImarily a reactionary one based on the historical lack of response to the gospel by Native people.

Quite often action based on a reaction seems to be valid rationale for trying to improve a situation. Relief pitchers are brought in to a baseball game when the coach determines the starter is losing control of his pitching arm and the flow of the game. A pinch hitter is brought in to bat for a teammate who has fallen into a hitting slump, all with the aim of correcting the current challenge while seeking to gain the advantage over their opponents. Sometimes, however, it does not improve the situation. The same can be said of reactionary efforts like that of the *Redeeming of Culture* movement.

Reactionary movements tend to track towards error as they seek to change things up. As they attempt to correct a problem, an overreaction often occurs when their answers move the pendulum from one extreme side to the other. This is exactly what the *Redeeming of Culture* movement has done. You can't solve one unbiblical problem by imposing an unbiblical solution.

Yes, there have been mistakes done in the past in the name of Christ. God honoring solutions will only be found when the Church steadfastly stands on the inerrant truth of God's Word.

History suggests that the non-believing world will normally side with relative truth as will those who embrace a low view of Scripture. If the authority of Scripture is of any importance to the Church in these last days, those who maintain a strong commitment to it must add their voices by weighing in on the theological issues of the day. The importance of that cannot be overstated.

Joshua had it right when he challenged Israel concerning the spiritual choices they were facing and his words are especially relevant for indigenous believers in Christ today because of our historical animism.

He says in Joshua 24:15;

*But if serving the Lord seems undesirable to you, then choose for yourselves this day whom you will serve, whether the gods your ancestors served beyond the Euphrates, or the gods of the Amorites, in whose land you are living. But as for me and my household, we will serve the Lord.*

Joshua articulates that every human culture is faced with three eternity altering options. First, there is the option of choosing to follow the gods of that culture's ancestors. This is the way of those who choose to follow traditional religions within the tribes.

Second, there will be those who choose to serve the gods in the land they are now living in. Such would be the case of indigenous people like ours who choose to wallow in the sin-stained culture of North America's larger dominate society.

These two sub-cultural groups need to acknowledge the presence of one other group of people within their communities. The third group are the Bible believing followers of Jesus Christ. They are the ones Joshua spoke of who choose to serve the Lord today as he and his family did in their generation.

That group consists of those who have been redeemed out of every tribe, language, people and nation. It is this redeemed community who choose to live their lives in alignment with the principles of a higher Kingdom, the Kingdom of God. It is often a maligned group, because it represents the only Hope for mankind as articulated in the pages of God's Holy Word.

That is why the Scriptures tell us in 1 Corinthians 1:18;

> *For the message of the cross is foolishness to those who are perishing, but to us who are being saved it is the power of God.*

If God's Word is absolute universal truth then we need to set our objections aside and give it a second look. We need to ask some serious questions about how it affects our lives. What other book in human history has survived so many nations and people groups trying to silence it or kill it off? As my colleague, Dr. Ravi Zacharias is often found stating, *Scripture always seems to have a way of rising up and outliving its own pallbearers!*

The exclusive claims of Scripture point to Jesus Christ as not just a great man, but the God-man who transcended heaven and earth, who came down to our level to pay the sacrifice for our sins, be buried, and rise again on the third day.

Who else do you know that has the power over death, my friend? Who else has come up out of the grave under His own power after three dead days? He's worth taking another look at. His claims need to be considered. His sacrifice and total forgiveness for you, if accepted, will bring to you not only life eternal but life abundant here on earth!

So, what does the revealed Scriptures have to say about our origins, both individually and corporately? What does the Bible have to say about the multitude of cultures spanning the globe? How did they arrive at their locations with such divergent faiths, beliefs, and practices?

More importantly, how do we as Christian indigenous people live out our faith while living in communities that by and large reject the Savior and His exclusive message?

It is time to transition from *defining the issues* to *discovering the truth*.

If every person living today were to hit the rewind button and go back far enough in human history, we would run into each other on the plains of Shinar as recorded in Genesis 11:1-9;

> *Now the whole world had one language and a common speech. As people moved eastward, they found a plain in Shinar and settled there. They said to each other, "Come, let's make bricks and bake them thoroughly." They used brick instead of stone, and tar for mortar. Then they said, "Come, let us build ourselves a city, with a tower that reaches to the heavens, so that we may make a name for ourselves; otherwise we will be scattered over the face of the whole earth." But the LORD came down to see the city and the tower the people were building. The LORD said, "If as one people speaking the same language they have begun to do this, then nothing they plan to do will be impossible for them. Come, let us go down and confuse their language so they will not understand each other." So the LORD scattered them from there over all the earth,*

*and they stopped building the city. That is why it was called Babel—because there the LORD confused the language of the whole world. From there the LORD scattered them over the face of the whole earth.*

Imagine that! We all have a common ancestry and a common original culture that is shared inclusively by every man, woman, and child now walking on Planet Earth! This stands in sharp contrast to what the myriad of cultures has to say about their own origins. It again begs the question; *Which truth is truth?*

To my traditional friends, many will undoubtedly reject the biblical account in favor of relative truth that differs from tribe to tribe. But in doing so, one has to reject the authority of the Scripture, which is, *God-breathed and is useful for teaching, rebuking, correcting and training in righteousness (2 Timothy 3:16).*

There was not only an original culture, but there was an original language as well. Now the Bible doesn't say what that original language was. I can only imagine it was Ojibwe!

Regardless, there are some important transcendent truths that help establish the biblical anatomy of human cultures.

Scripture highlights two key reasons our common ancestors decided to stop on the plains of Shinar and build a city and tower that reached to the heavens. First, was *so that we would make a name for ourselves (v. 4a).* Secondly, so that *otherwise, we would be scattered over the face of the whole earth (v. 4b).*

Think about this with me for a moment. If our common ancestors were the only people group in existence at the time, to whom were they going to make a name? Who were they trying to impress? All they could do was impress themselves! What do you think is at the core of that kind of attitude? The only answer is PRIDE!

Pride has always been the bitter enemy of all things holy and godly. Pride says I am *Numero Uno* and nobody better get in my way! Pride says, *I want what you have and I'll take it from you whether you want me to or not.*

The core of unregenerate human behavior is evident in every beautiful little baby turned monster who has matured enough to utter or even think the words, *MINE*! Watch out as that little one grows up continuing to exhibit prideful behavior.

Pride is also at the heart of every human conflict between warring tribes and nations.

> C.S. Lewis noted, *Pride is spiritual cancer: it eats up the very possibility of love, or contentment, or even common sense.*[28]

---

[28] C. S. Lewis: *Mere Christianity*, p. 124

*Indigenous Faith*

> A. W. Tozer once stated, *The heart of the world is breaking under this load of pride and pretense. There is no release from our burden apart from the meekness of Christ.*[29]
>
> As the great English journalist, G.K. Chesterton humorously noted, *The cosmos is about the smallest hole that a man can hide his head in.*[30]

My tribe is known by several names. We are often identified as either *Chippewa* or *Ojibwe*, both of which are given names. The real name of our people, the one we use to identify ourselves is *Anishinabe*. Translated it means, *THE people* (emphasis on the word THE)! Maybe that's why I suggested the original language on the plains of Shinar was Ojibwe!

Then I married a Navajo. Now that's not the real name for her people. They refer to themselves as *Dine'*. Guess what that name means? THE people!

Navigate this world from pole to pole, and you'll find each tribe identifying themselves as THE people, or the ORIGINAL people, or in some other similar way. If you do not find it in the name look a bit further, and you'll find it in their view of themselves in relation to those other nations around them. Pride is found in the DNA of every human culture in existence.

---

[29] A. W. Tozer: *The Pursuit of God* p. 151

[30] G. K. Chesterton, *Orthodoxy* p. 35

The second reason for stopping and setting up shop on the plains of Shinar was to ensure that our common ancestors would not be scattered throughout the earth. So, what's that all about, and what does that attitude uncover in our mutual ancestors? The reason can only be described as *disobedience to God!*

Why?

When God made original man and woman, He issued the following instruction to them as recorded in Genesis 1:28a;

> *God blessed them and said to them, "Be fruitful and increase in number; fill the earth and subdue it."*

Depending on which translation you use, there are over 31,100 verses contained in the entire Bible. You can't even get past Genesis 1:28 before you find God's marching orders to our original ancestors! There is an important reason for this showing up so early in human history.

*Fill the earth*, He stated! Do not stop, but scatter! That is not just a suggestion but an explicit command from the very One who created our original ancestors, Adam and Eve. If anyone had known God as Creator and the importance of obeying His words, it would have been these two!

But sin they did, and cursed they became.

In Genesis 3:14-15, a primitive form of the gospel was introduced by God to remedy this curse which has affected all mankind ever since;

> *The Lord God said to the serpent, Because you have done this, cursed are you above all livestock and above all beasts of the field; on your belly you shall go, and dust you shall eat all the days of your life. I will put enmity between you and the woman, and between your offspring and her offspring; he shall bruise your head, and you shall bruise his heel.*

From this point on, Genesis records the expansion of the human family in chapters 3-10. One doesn't get very far before finding out how mankind was faring in the eyes of the One who had created them. It is not a good report card, for sure, as Genesis 6:5-8 records;

> *The Lord saw how great the wickedness of the human race had become on the earth, and that every inclination of the thoughts of the human heart was only evil all the time. The Lord regretted that he had made human beings on the earth, and his heart was deeply troubled. So the Lord said, "I will wipe from the face of the earth the human race I have created—and with them the animals, the birds and the creatures that move along the ground—for I regret that I have made them." But Noah found favor in the eyes of the Lord.*

Scripture reveals the story of the flood and the universal judgment of God that ensued. A horrible wiping out of all mankind took place, save for the faithfulness of God to Noah and his family. Representation of the animal and bird kingdoms were there as well. As the waters receded, God's reset button for earth was pushed.

What did God say to Noah and his family as they disembarked their cruise ship? He said to them in Genesis 9:1-7;

> *Then God blessed Noah and his sons, saying to them, "Be fruitful and increase in number and fill the earth. The fear and dread of you will fall on all the beasts of the earth, and on all the birds in the sky, on every creature that moves along the ground, and on all the fish in the sea; they are given into your hands. Everything that lives and moves about will be food for you. Just as I gave you the green plants, I now give you everything. "But you must not eat meat that has its lifeblood still in it. And for your lifeblood I will surely demand an accounting. I will demand an accounting from every animal. And from each human being, too, I will demand an accounting for the life of another human being. "Whoever sheds human blood, by humans shall their blood be shed; for in the image of God has God made mankind. As for you, be fruitful and increase in number; multiply on the earth and increase upon it."*

Did you notice it? What God said to Adam and Eve He now says once again to Noah and his descendants. He told them in v.1 to, *be fruitful and increase in number and fill the earth.* He repeats himself in v.7 when He states, *As for you, be fruitful and increase in number; multiply on the earth and increase upon it.*

God's direct instruction to them was the same expectation He had for those encamped on the plains of Shinar. But that edict was cast aside on the altar of convenient disobedience by pride filled members of our mutual family tree. That's why the rationale for staying on the plains of Shinar was so offensive to God. They knew His charge to Adam and Eve, and they knew His renewed charge to Noah and his family—to scatter and not stay put. That's blatant disobedience to God.

So, there you have it.

The Genesis 11 passage also confirms the fact that it was God, Himself, who confused the languages just prior to shooing us off Babel's tower and just before He began mankind's relocation process.

If we're honest with ourselves, a realistic appraisal of the introduction of the languages by God can only have one accurate rationale behind it. It was God's response to the pride and arrogance of our common ancestors and not a reward for it.

Language has become very important to all people. We value our native languages as one of the uniquenesses that sets us apart from the rest of the world. A preserved native tongue is also endearingly referred to in missiological terms as the *heart language* of the people. But let us be clear, while our *heart languages* were given to us by God, they were given primarily as one of ways He chose to deal with our ancestor's pride and disobedience.

After the initial outpouring of tongues, the dispersing of the nations ensued.

This diaspora was not instantaneous, though. It happened over the course of centuries, as God dispersed what was to become all the nations of the world. This includes all the nations that have been completely wiped off the planet due to wars, diseases, and other manifestations of pride still found to be in the DNA of every sin-stained culture.

Go with me from Genesis 11 to Acts 17:22-28, where the Apostle Paul is speaking to the Athenian elite about not only our God given *languages*, but our God given *locations*;

> *"The God who made the world and everything in it is the Lord of heaven and earth and does not live in temples built by human hands. And he is not served by human hands, as if he needed anything. Rather, he himself gives everyone life and breath and everything else. From one man he made all the nations, that they should inhabit the whole earth; and he marked out their appointed times in history and the boundaries of their lands. God did this so that they would seek him and perhaps reach out for him and find him, though he is not far from any one of us. 'For*

> *in him we live and move and have our being.' As some of your own poets have said, 'We are his offspring.'*

The biblical case can be made of God giving the nations their languages and locations, because there is Scriptural proof from the texts referenced above. In later chapters we will look more closely at the implications of this important passage in Acts, because it is one of great consequence and relevance to indigenous people worldwide.

But for now, and relevant to this chapter's focus, is the question, *Is there clear and compelling evidence, from Scripture, that God gave all the nations their unique cultures and religious paths that bear His blessing and sanction?*

I can't find it in the Word. Can you? In my over forty years delving into biblical truth, I've yet to find chapter and verse that clearly states such. And that is problematic for syncretists, because key theological positions are being taken from presuppositions that do not have a biblical basis to rest upon.

It reminds me of an anonymous quote I once read;

*Wonderful things in the Bible I see. Most of them put there by you and by me!*

One of the presuppositions embraced by the syncretism camp is that in the process of the scattering of the nations, God showed up along the way and gave them their cultural ways, ceremonies, and traditions that enjoy His sanction and blessing. One can hold to this position, but it has to be based on something other than biblical sources. In fact, in order to hold to that presupposition, one has to reject clear biblical doctrine articulated in Psalms 147:19-20;

> *He has revealed his word to Jacob, his laws and decrees to Israel. He has done this for no other nation; they do not know his laws...*

Compare the presupposition that God has *done this for all other nations* against clear biblical truth that states God *has done this for no other nation,* and you see that this theological house has been built on quicksand! Furthermore, contrast this position against what Scripture clearly teaches about God's evaluation of all nations as outlined in the important passage of Romans 1:18-32. We will be looking at this passage in greater detail later on.

One of the Canadian leaders of the *Redeeming of Culture* movement articulated this presupposition rather clearly in a radio interview done a few years ago. The statement says this about indigenous cultures worldwide;

> *God is now calling forth from among the indigenous communities of the world that good deposit which He has made in them of their cultures, their languages, their*

> *musical expressions and all that sort of thing ... as an expression of praise and worship unto Himself.*[31]

In that same interview, this leader further stated,

> *There's a myth that we have labored under for centuries in indigenous communities and the myth is that we are a godless heathen people. And yet all brings glory to God in its own special way, and that's true of human beings and cultures as well.*[32]

Scripture tells us that apart from Christ all nations are godless and hopelessly lost. Ephesians 2:12 states;

> *...remember that at that time you were separate from Christ, excluded from citizenship in Israel and foreigners to the covenants of the promise, without hope and without God in the world.*

God's Holy Word cannot be any clearer! All nations are *without hope and without God in this world!* What enlightenment do these folks have that gives their positions authority over Scripture? What special revelation from God do they have when they emphatically state, *And yet all brings glory to God in its own special way, and that's true of human beings*

---

[31] Terry LeBlanc, *Word to the World*, show #542

[32] ibid

*and cultures as well.* A bold assertion for sure and clearly false teaching.

This movement has produced an emerging indigenous based academic organization called NAIITS (North American Institute for Indigenous Theological Studies). It has been impacting academia with its cultural based focus on theological studies across North America and beyond. The notion that God has invested Himself in every human culture is the highlighted theme offered by NAIITS in its official website's vision statement. It reads;

> *Our desire is to see men and women journey down the road of a living heart relationship with Jesus in a transformative way – one which does not require the rejection of their Creator-given social and cultural identity.*[33]

I am still looking for the passages of Scripture that affirm *Creator-given social and cultural identity* for all nations as a biblical reality.

Maintaining a high view of Scripture leaves me no option but to look to the Word of God for confirmation. The only way to embrace such a presupposition is to take the low road down to a low view of Scripture. A high view of Scripture requires we find within the pages of the Book actual texts that show that to be the case. The problem is

---

[33] http://naiits.com/vision/

any student of the Bible is hard pressed to find support of this position, because those texts simply do not exist.

My question to the scholars and academia in our institutions of Christian higher education is, *Where are the voices that, at minimum, raise their collective theological concerns and ask critical questions based on Scriptural truth, even when it is culturally uncomfortable to do so?*

Animism's trick is its ability to hide spirituality behind the colorful blanket of culture. Yet, in that hiding, it actually shouts loud and clear to its followers, *follow me!* You really can't separate the two. In the North American indigenous community, culture is our spirituality and spirituality is our culture. To raise theological questions in that cultural context is akin to challenging or even disparaging a people's culture and traditions. That certainly seems not the thing to do in this present day and age.

When the syncretists use Scriptural texts, they are often given over to an interpretation that does not convey the original intent of the passage. Something other than a grammatico-historical hermeneutic is employed to interpret it. A more culturally based hermeneutic fits their purposes well, because culture becomes the prism by which Scripture is interpreted. Anything goes with that kind of theology. An abandonment of historical universal truth gives way to *itching ear* doctrines which Scripture says finds its roots in the demonic realm, as 2 Timothy 4:3 states;

*For the time will come when people will not put up with sound doctrine. Instead, to suit their own desires, they will gather around them a great number of teachers to say what their itching ears want to hear.*

### Israel's Uniqueness

As you leave Genesis 11, chapter 12 begins with the call of God to Abram (who later would be called Abraham). Scripture states in Genesis 12:1-3;

*The LORD had said to Abram, "Go from your country, your people and your father's household to the land I will show you. I will make you into a great nation and I will bless you; I will make your name great, and you will be a blessing. I will bless those who bless you, and whoever curses you I will curse, and all peoples on earth will be blessed through you."*

From this point on to the end of the Old Testament, a very clear and compelling case is made of God choosing to bless Abram and his descendants with a very special blessing and calling. He affirms that out of his seed will be born a great and mighty nation. This part of earth's humanity became known as Israel. Those who stand with this nation will be blessed, and those who do not will bear God's curse. It ends with this great Messianic promise, *and all peoples on earth will be blessed through you (v.3).*

All the peoples on the earth would be blessed through Israel, because they were the nation through whom God would send his One and only Son, Jesus the Christ, who would fatally bruise the head of the serpent, Satan, the deceiver of all nations.

This was the beginning of just one of the growing list of human cultures that were forming post Shinar. What an important people group Abram's seed would become. Israel was the only nation that God chose to give a unique and special blessing. They were the only ones He established a unique Covenant with, placed a special responsibility upon, and to whom He would visit with *special revelation*.

Deuteronomy 7:7 tells us;

*The Lord did not set his affection on you and choose you because you were more numerous than other peoples, for you were the fewest of all peoples.*

As I noted in *Whiteman's Gospel,* Israel was chosen by God not because of their inherent strength, but because of their incredible weakness. They were not the largest people group spanning the globe, but were the fewest of the few.

There are many people groups that to this day hold a deep seeded hatred against Israel. The Middle East is a firestorm of animosity as this tiny nation continues to serve God's purposes even to this day.

Throughout the Old Testament we learn about the unique relationship between Israel and God. It explains how God gave Israel their unique culture, diet, morality, and religion.

God's relationship with Israel specifically, and not the other nations, is poignantly articulated by God through the prophet Amos. Amos 3:1-2 states;

> *Hear this word, people of Israel, the word the Lord has spoken against you—against the whole family I brought up out of Egypt: "You only have I chosen of all the families of the earth; therefore I will punish you for all your sins."*

With that unique blessing came responsibilities and judgements by God when Israel compromised, disobeyed, and syncretized. Regardless of the theme of judgement noted in Amos, there is this clear statement that we should not miss;

> *You only have I chosen of all the families of the earth...*

Through God's powerful manifestation to Moses on Mount Sinai, He gave Israel His *Top Ten List*. Scripture records these Ten Commandments in Exodus 20:3-17;

1. *You shall have no other gods before me.*
2. *You shall not make for yourself an image in the form of anything in heaven above or on the earth beneath or in the waters below. You shall not bow down to them or worship them; for I, the Lord your God, am a jealous God, punishing the children for the sin of the parents to the third and fourth generation of those who hate me, but showing love to a thousand generations of those who love me and keep my commandments.*
3. *You shall not misuse the name of the Lord your God, for the Lord will not hold anyone guiltless who misuses his name.*
4. *Remember the Sabbath day by keeping it holy. Six days you shall labor and do all your work, but the seventh day is a sabbath to the Lord your God. On it you shall not do any work, neither you, nor your son or daughter, nor your male or female servant, nor your animals, nor any foreigner residing in your towns. For in six days the Lord made the heavens and the earth, the sea, and all that is in them, but he rested on the seventh day. Therefore the Lord blessed the Sabbath day and made it holy.*
5. *Honor your father and your mother, so that you may live long in the land the Lord your God is giving you.*
6. *You shall not murder.*
7. *You shall not commit adultery.*
8. *You shall not steal.*

9. *You shall not give false testimony against your neighbor.*
10. *You shall not covet your neighbor's house. You shall not covet your neighbor's wife, or his male or female servant, his ox or donkey, or anything that belongs to your neighbor.*

These Commandments set the holy standards for Israel. Also, it is through these decrees God imparted a universal moral compass into all His created humanity. Upon these Commandments the laws of many nations have been established.

Unfortunately, America's current and ever increasingly pagan culture has chosen to amputate these God given Commandments by removing them from our schools, courthouses, and other public places. What we now find in its place are metal detectors, school shootings, murders, and rapes occurring on an all too regular basis. Daily reviews of our community newspapers and other media outlets are constant reminders of how depraved mankind continues to be.

We read further of God's admonitions to tiny Israel as they interacted with the other nations around them. It gives us a window into God's heart on how He views all nations who suffer under the curse of sin.

The Lord tells Israel to be careful in its dealings with the other nations, because He does not approve, nor endorse, their religions, faiths, and practices. He doesn't mince words when he states to Israel, in Deuteronomy 12:2-4;

> *Destroy completely all the places on the high mountains, on the hills and under every spreading tree, where the nations you are dispossessing worship their gods. Break down their altars, smash their sacred stones and burn their Asherah poles in the fire; cut down the idols of their gods and wipe out their names from those places. You must not worship the LORD your God in their way.*

Do you see it? *You must not worship the LORD your God in their way*!

That doesn't agree with the presupposition of the syncretists about God's acceptance of the ways of the other nations!

He continues His thoughts to Israel later on in the chapter as He further emphasizes the point in Deuteronomy 12:29-31;

> *The LORD your God will cut off before you the nations you are about to invade and dispossess. But when you have driven them out and settled in their land, and after they have been destroyed before you, be careful not to be ensnared by inquiring about their gods, saying, "How do these nations serve their gods? We will do the same." You must not worship the LORD your God in their way,*

*because in worshiping their gods, they do all kinds of detestable things the LORD hates. They even burn their sons and daughters in the fire as sacrifices to their gods.*

One of the key things that angered God back then was when the Gentile nations built for themselves sacred objects, idols, and began detestable practices and ways of worshipping these graven images. Israel didn't fare much better as they compromised by incorporating into their own God-given worship a blending of these practices.

So, did Israel obey God's commands? It depends on what part of their historical timeline you are looking at. There were times of obedience to God, and there were times of great disobedience. When they obeyed His instructions it resulted in the blessing and favor of God. When they disobeyed, the judgment of God fell heavily on Israel when they gave way to compromise and syncretized. A painfully perfect example of this is recorded in Psalms 106:35-39 where it states;

*...but they mingled with the nations and adopted their customs. They worshiped their idols, which became a snare to them. They sacrificed their sons and their daughters to false gods. They shed innocent blood, the blood of their sons and daughters, whom they sacrificed to the idols of Canaan, and the land was desecrated by their blood. They*

*defiled themselves by what they did; by their deeds they prostituted themselves.*

Imagine, God's chosen people, defiling themselves by sacrificing their children to the false gods of Canaan!

In *Whiteman's Gospel*, I shared my heart on the issue of modern American paganism more in depth. I connected the dots between the Old Testament gods and goddesses such as Asherah (Ashtoreth), Chemosh and Molek, with modern Western culture and practices. It is important to remember, though, that Israel suffered consequences when they engaged in such pagan worship.

In I Kings 11:30-33, it says;

*[30] Ahijah took hold of the new cloak he was wearing and tore it into twelve pieces. Then he said to Jeroboam, "Take ten pieces for yourself, for this is what the LORD, the God of Israel, says: 'See, I am going to tear the kingdom out of Solomon's hand and give you ten tribes. But for the sake of my servant David and the city of Jerusalem, which I have chosen out of all the tribes of Israel, he will have one tribe. I will do this because they have forsaken me and worshiped Ashtoreth the goddess of the Sidonians, Chemosh the god of the Moabites, and Molek the god of the Ammonites, and have not walked in obedience to me, nor done what is right in my eyes, nor kept my decrees and laws as David, Solomon's father, did.*

Asherah worship involved an *Asherah Pole*, where nude women would dance around, enticing the worshippers with their sexual prodding and teasing. Prostitution was at the center of such worship, and Israel fell head first into it like all the other nations around them. That same worship is engaged today in strip clubs around the world. The Asherah pole continues to draw men and women alike into its pagan worship.

With the convenience and privacy of the internet, modern Old Testament pagan worship is showing up in basements, bedrooms, and other private places in homes along with establishments around the world.

Slick Madison Avenue advertising continues to promote such worship in modern American society. The insatiable appetite for sexual deviancy noted in Romans 1 marches on. It has found a home not only in modern Western culture, but in third world nations and among all other societies under sin's grotesque grip. And that is just Asherah worship.

Let's not forget about her good friends, Chemosh and Molek!

The gods Chemosh and Molek of the Moabites and Ammonites were hollow metal gods formed with their arms outstretched. Men would build fires inside these hollow metal gods until their metal burned red hot with unimaginable heat. Worshippers would then bring their innocent babies and lay them into the burning arms of these horrific gods. They would watch their precious screaming babies burn to death right before their own eyes as their blood flowed down to the ground.

> *Two pagan gods were particularly detestable, Chemosh the pagan god of the Moabites and Molech the pagan god of the Ammonites, because their worship called for the sacrifice of infants.*
>
> *Topheth, meaning "place of fire," was a site of worship for Molech; however, its primitive root word "toph" meant "playing or beating a percussion instrument such as a timbrel, tambourine, or drum". Scholars believe that it was possible that percussion instruments were used to drown out the sounds of infants as they were burned alive.*[34]

It left God no other choice but to render the scathing indictment of Israel as noted above in Psalms 106:35-39.

It does not take a rocket scientist to connect the dots of these horrific gods with modern society's insatiable appetite for the continued sacrifice of innocent children through abortion. Around sixty million children since *Roe vs. Wade* have been laid into the molten arms of Molek and Chemosh, as their innocent blood spills onto the floors of provider offices across the land. Infanticide is now being offered as

---

[34] http://helpmewithbiblestudy.org/8Sin/IdolotryTophethBeatingDrums.aspx#sthash.b3ydWxU9.dpbs

the ultimate sacrifice, causing babies who have been either partially or fully delivered to be put to death as well.

As a Native American, an indigenous person of this great land, I have to go on record to call this country to account for the same thing Israel did, the *[sacrificing] of [our] sons and [our] daughters to false gods. [We] have shed innocent blood, the blood of [our] sons and daughters, [whom we as a nation] have sacrificed to the idols of Canaan, and the land [of America has been] desecrated by their blood* (parenthetical inserts added).

Please stop here and ponder this reality. What is the Spirit of God saying to us individually and to our nation? If this does not shake us, I do not know what will.

To the syncretists among us, I urge you to reconsider your positions, presuppositions, and convictions and see where compromise has taken you. Learn the lessons of God's people, Israel! This is serious business with eternal consequences.

May we respond to God with *godly sorrow that leads to repentance (2 Cor. 7:10)*. He will hear us as we repent, forgive us of our sin, and bring healing to our land as 2 Chronicles 7:14 says;

*If my people, who are called by my name, will humble themselves and pray and seek my face and turn from their wicked ways, then I will hear from heaven, and I will forgive their sin and will heal their land.*

*Chapter Seven*

# LESSONS FROM EZEKIEL

THE BOOK OF EZEKIEL IS AN IMPORTANT OLD TESTAMENT book. Ezekiel's name means *strengthened by God.* It is a fitting name for this prophet because Ezekiel needed God's strength to confront the many sins of Israel in their exiled state. God gave him visions, prophecies, parables, signs, and symbols to proclaim His truth to a nation of compromisers and syncretizers.

During this time Israel welcomed the ways, worship, and sacred objects of the nations around them and made them their own. These actions did not bring the favor of God but resulted in His judgement.

God states to Israel in Ezekiel 16:47;

*You not only followed their ways and copied their detestable practices, but in all your ways you soon became more depraved than they.*

Israel's sins have been shared by compromisers all throughout human history.

Copy is a good word to describe why syncretists do what they do in much the same way a duplicate is made of an original document on a copy machine.

The original document is the form, practice, or sacred object birthed and practiced in the culture from which it emanates. Syncretists do not use the original, but choose to copy that form, practice, or sacred object. They redirect and incorporate it into their own spirituality and worship of God. It is a misguided attempt at *redeeming* those things based on a belief that in doing so, God is pleased.

If it did not result in the blessing and favor of God when Israel did it, how can one believe it will receive God's blessing and favor now?

Notice what the last part of the verse stated. It says, *in all your ways you soon became more depraved than they.* Israel was not just as bad as the others, they actually became *more depraved* then the nations that owned the originals!

When our ancestors left Shinar's plains, they left with a mutual understanding of the One true God as revealed to them in Genesis chapters 1-10. They also left with the nasty luggage of pride and disobedience that is still firmly entrenched in the heart and soul of all mankind. Because of that I am left with no other option than to say that the depravity of man is the foundation on which all world religions, save Judaism and Christianity, have been birthed.

Embracing this reality can only be arrived at if we believe the Bible says what it means and means what it says.

Paul's letter to the Romans clearly states this.

Romans 1:18–23 says;

*The wrath of God is being revealed from heaven against all the godlessness and wickedness of people, who suppress the truth by their wickedness, since what may be known about God is plain to them, because God has made it plain to them. For since the creation of the world God's invisible qualities—his eternal power and divine nature—have been clearly seen, being understood from what has been made, so that people are without excuse. For although they knew God, they neither glorified him as God nor gave thanks to him, but their thinking became futile and their foolish hearts were darkened. Although they claimed to be wise, they became fools and exchanged the glory of the immortal God for images made to look like a mortal human being and birds and animals and reptiles.*

Romans 1:25 summarizes the dilemma faced by every nation;

*They exchanged the truth about God for a lie, and worshiped and served created things rather than the Creator— who is forever praised. Amen.*

*Indigenous Faith*

In Ezekiel 8, God singles out *the leaders of the house of Israel* in His indictment of their willful disobedience. I shudder to think what false teachers will face when they stand before Almighty God to give an account for not only the lies they believed but for the number of people they led down their well-traveled roads.

Let the Word of God speak for itself, then compare the practices back then with what the syncretists practice and promote today.

Ezekiel 8 states;

*In the sixth year, in the sixth month on the fifth day, while I was sitting in my house and the elders of Judah were sitting before me, the hand of the Sovereign LORD came on me there. I looked, and I saw a figure like that of a man. From what appeared to be his waist down he was like fire, and from there up his appearance was as bright as glowing metal. He stretched out what looked like a hand and took me by the hair of my head. The Spirit lifted me up between Earth and heaven and in visions of God he took me to Jerusalem, to the entrance of the north gate of the inner court, where the idol that provokes to jealousy stood. And there before me was the glory of the God of Israel, as in the vision I had seen in the plain.*

*Then he said to me, "Son of man, look toward the north." So I looked, and in the entrance north of the gate of the altar I saw this idol of jealousy.*

*And he said to me, "Son of man, do you see what they are doing—the utterly detestable things the Israelites are doing here, things that will drive me far from my sanctuary? But you will see things that are even more detestable."*

*Then he brought me to the entrance to the court. I looked, and I saw a hole in the wall. He said to me, "Son of man, now dig into the wall." So I dug into the wall and saw a doorway there.*

*And he said to me, "Go in and see the wicked and detestable things they are doing here." So I went in and looked, and I saw portrayed all over the walls all kinds of crawling things and unclean animals and all the idols of Israel. In front of them stood seventy elders of Israel, and Jaazaniah son of Shaphan was standing among them. Each had a censer in his hand, and a fragrant cloud of incense was rising.*

*He said to me, "Son of man, have you seen what the elders of Israel are doing in the darkness, each at the shrine of his own idol? They say, 'The LORD does not see us; the*

*LORD has forsaken the land.'" Again, he said, "You will see them doing things that are even more detestable."*

*Then he brought me to the entrance of the north gate of the house of the LORD, and I saw women sitting there, mourning the god Tammuz. He said to me, "Do you see this, son of man? You will see things that are even more detestable than this."*

*He then brought me into the inner court of the house of the LORD, and there at the entrance to the temple, between the portico and the altar, were about twenty-five men. With their backs toward the temple of the LORD and their faces toward the east, they were bowing down to the sun in the east.*

*He said to me, "Have you seen this, son of man? Is it a trivial matter for the people of Judah to do the detestable things they are doing here? Must they also fill the land with violence and continually arouse my anger? Look at them putting the branch to their nose! Therefore I will deal with them in anger; I will not look on them with pity or spare them. Although they shout in my ears, I will not listen to them."*

The leaders of the House of Israel brought into the temple of the Lord *idols that provoked God to jealousy*. Bible scholars tend to agree that these idols were the Babylonian god Baal, and the goddess Asherah, whom we have already met earlier.

Why does this seem to be such a serious thing to God? I think it best to let Him answer that question directly.

A brief return to the Ten Commandments is necessary to once again hear His heart. God's *top two* of His *top ten list* reads as follows. *Have no other gods before me, and do not make any graven images.*

This was not just a corporate issue for Israel. It was also a personal one. Israel was instructed by God to not bring sacred objects into the sanctuary of God or into their homes as well.

Deuteronomy 7:25-26 says;

*The images of their gods you are to burn in the fire. Do not covet the silver and gold on them, and do not take it for yourselves, or you will be ensnared by it, for it is detestable to the LORD your God. Do not bring a detestable thing into your house or you, like it, will be set apart for destruction. Regard it as vile and utterly detest it, for it is set apart for destruction.*

God's Word is clear! The same admonition holds true for us as indigenous people who are now in the family of God. He tells us, *No other gods, and no graven images*!

On the personal side we as indigenous believers in Christ must not keep or bring into our homes sacred objects of any culture, whatever they may be.

Why? Because the clear teaching of Scripture confirms these sacred objects are not pleasing to God and should not be to His redeemed people as well. These graven images and the spiritual power indwelt by them will often be manifested in our homes, families, and personal lives. They cause great fear and danger to a compromising Christian. All too often we bring upon ourselves our own tormentors when we choose to keep the gods and sacred things of our people in our possession.

Unexplainable manifestations in our homes are often tied to the supernatural resident in sacred objects. Doors opening and closing on their own, the presence of someone or something in the room, or even dishes flying off the shelves point to the supernatural power in sacred things. These are some of the experiences that LaDonna and I have dealt with in ministry to those who have sought our help.

This supernatural power can render our bodies susceptible to illness and disease. Often it leaves medical professionals scratching their heads as they wonder why these symptoms are manifesting themselves, while remaining medically unexplainable.

It is akin to putting raw hamburger out on the deck on a hot summer day. It will not be long before the flies show up. We will pay the price if we allow sacred objects to hang around allowing the demonic spirits to do their dirty work.

On the corporate side, *Indigenous Faith* compels us to not redeem any sacred objects of our past. Do not even attempt to bring them into the house of God. We must not seek to copy and reuse them for a more culturally acceptable way to worship. All that does is *drive God far from His sanctuary and make us more detestable than they!*

Remember, God's review of mankind in Genesis 6 was that *the thoughts of his heart were only evil continually.* That being the case, syncretists have to answer an important question. *What changed after Genesis 6 when suddenly God's review of mankind improved enough for Him to bless and invest Himself in the new cultures that emerged post Shinar?*

If all cultures contain *that good deposit which He has made in them of their cultures, their languages, their musical expressions and all that sort of thing,* when exactly did the Lord make that deposit? Such an earth-shattering event worthy of Scripture's mention should be found in God's Word. It would have happened somewhere between the flood and when Israel brought Baal and Asherah into the sanctuary of God. Unfortunately for the syncretists, no biblical account exists.

This leads us to the question, *What are the sacred objects of our people?*

Because there are great differences among tribal cultures, there is not a single answer to this incredibly important question. Sacred objects can differ from tribe to tribe.

In *Boundary Lines,* we offered a good working definition of sacred objects.

> *Sacred objects are objects used specifically in spirit worship or animistic practices. They are often used as mediators between man and the spirit realm. In this role, they are indwelt by spiritual beings or powers. Sacred objects can be animate (living) or inanimate (non-living) objects made animate by indwelling demonic powers. Culturally, it is normally taboo to use sacred objects in common ways, as they are reserved for specific purposes and rituals.[35]*

We also offered a fairly comprehensive sampling of what some of the animate and inanimate sacred objects of our Native people are.

### Examples of Animate (living) Sacred Objects[36]
*Any animal, bird, fish, plant, or other living being has the potential of being a sacred object, if a particular tribe has ascribed to it spiritual significance and power. Also, if any*

---

[35] Ibid, p.34.

[36] Ibid, p.39.

animate object is dedicated through an animistic ritual or ceremony, it then becomes a sacred object.

<u>Examples of Inanimate Sacred Objects</u>
Any geographical feature (mountains, stones, rivers, valleys, etc.) that a particular tribe has ascribed to it spiritual significance and power is to be considered a sacred object. A location where a non-biblical vision has occurred has become, to the recipient, his family and potentially their tribe as a whole, depending on that tribe's traditional theology, a sacred place. In some instances, due to the "pan-Indian movement" sacred places, objects, etc., of other tribes are viewed as sacred to another tribe that has had no previous exposure or acceptance of those ways in their traditional system of beliefs. Kivas, sweat lodges, longhouses, tobacco, peyote tipis and sticks; smoke from cedar, sage, sweetgrass or other mediatory incenses are sacred objects. Fetish masks, drums, rattles, whistles, Kachina and Yeibechi dolls, carvings, bundles, medicine pouches, dream catchers, totem poles, are all sacred objects.

In the quote from Richard Twiss he noted that the pastor (implying a white missionary or pastor) told him his drum and other cultural paraphernalia was *full of idolatry.*

How did this pastor come to this understanding? Was it just another irresponsible and bigoted response from someone who did not understand or appreciate Native culture? Syncretists must acknowledge that this information has always been articulated and promoted by our Native traditional leaders and medicine men and women themselves!

A number of years ago Rev. Tom Claus presented a paper in which he shared quotes from Native traditional leaders defining some of the sacred objects of our people. The quotes are enlightening.

- Black Elk (Lakota);
  *Its round form (the drum) represents the universe, and its steady strong beat is the pulse, the heart, throbbing at the center of the universe. As the voice of Wakan Tanka (God), it stirs and helps us to understand the mystery and power of things.*

- White Buffalo Calf Woman (Lakota);
  *The pipe is very sacred and you must treat it as such. With this pipe you will send your voices to Wakan Tanka (God), your father and grandfather.*

- Iroquois belief in tobacco;
  *Tobacco is crumbled and strewn in holy places as an offering to the spirits. It is also sprinkled onto an open fire in sacrifice to the spirits. The smoke from tobacco is a means of communicating with the spirit*

world. The smoke carries our words and thoughts to the spirits.

- Tewa Leader on songs & dances;
  *The purpose of our ceremonies, songs and dances are not performed for fun as they are in the white man's world; they are more than that; they are the very essence of our lives. Even the smallest things may have enormous spiritual significance to an Indian.*

- A Kiowa elder on the drum;
  *All of our elders believe that the drum has medicinal powers; it makes you forget...makes you feel good... it enlightens you...and whatever obstacles that may be confronting you...it gives you that added strength to confront them. That's what the drum does for you. Many people dance and put their problems and their prayer requests on the drum. That is part of our life here, our Indian way of living.*

- Cree tribal singers on the drum;
  *The drum is sacred. The drum has its own spirit. We trust in the drum for everything.*[37]

Today's syncretism movement attempts to redeem Native drums as musical instruments to aid in a more

---
[37] Rev. H. Thomas Claus, CHIEF, Inc. www.CHIEF.org

*culturally appropriate worship.* The Native drum is clearly a sacred object and not just a musical instrument. As such, it must be subject to biblical scrutiny.

A Native drum is totally different from a Western style drum bought in some music store in Nashville, Tennessee. Western culture does not ascribe a highly-revered sacredness to its *Slingerland* or *Pearl* drum sets. They do not pray to it, treat it with supernatural spiritual reverence, or ascribe to it medicinal powers. It is simply a musical instrument. It is not a sacred object.

Over the years the *Redeeming of Culture* movement has attempted to posture this debate not as a sacred object dispute but only a musical instrument one. They suggest this is no different than the debate a century or so ago when the church was hotly contesting those who were bringing pianos into the church to accompany its worship.

The piano suffered from the reputation of being a *godless instrument* straight from the honky tonks and dance halls. It was perceived to be the *instrument of the devil,* because they were used to promote debauchery.

There is a problem with debating the issue from merely the musical instrument standpoint. Truth be told, organs and pianos have been, and continue to be, *spiritually neutral musical instruments*, and not the sacred objects of an animistic culture. As such, they have the potential of being used in God honoring ways of His worshiping church, regardless of the culture that seeks to utilize them. Sacred objects do not enjoy the same.

Look at where the church is at today. An organ is now considered a relic of the past, and the piano has been replaced with electronic keyboard synthesizers, guitars, drums, etc., in many contemporary worship services.

I get that clearly my friend and hope you do as well. Those involved in Native American spirituality have the drum front and center in their traditional theology and practices. The Cree singers articulated this position clearly. *The drum is sacred. The drum has its own spirit. We trust in the drum for everything.*

When Israel destroyed its sacred objects (i.e. Asherah poles) they didn't return from the bonfire to make new neutral Asherah poles to replace the sacred ones. The clear concept was to destroy and distance one's self from these objects, as outlined in the New Testament's doctrine of Separation.

2 Corinthians 6:14-16a says;

*Do not be yoked together with unbelievers. For what do righteousness and wickedness have in common? Or what fellowship can light have with darkness? What harmony is there between Christ and Belial? What does a believer have in common with an unbeliever? What agreement is there between the temple of God and idols?"*

King Josiah removed the Asherah poles and other sacred paraphernalia from the Temple of God. He did not go back to the Temple and order his craftsmen to make new neutral Asherah poles.

2 Kings 23:6-14 says;

*He took the Asherah pole from the temple of the Lord to the Kidron Valley outside Jerusalem and burned it there. He ground it to powder and scattered the dust over the graves of the common people. He also tore down the quarters of the male shrine prostitutes that were in the temple of the Lord, the quarters where women did weaving for Asherah.*

*Josiah brought all the priests from the towns of Judah and desecrated the high places, from Geba to Beersheba, where the priests had burned incense. He broke down the gateway at the entrance of the Gate of Joshua, the city governor, which was on the left of the city gate. Although the priests of the high places did not serve at the altar of the Lord in Jerusalem, they ate unleavened bread with their fellow priests.*

*He desecrated Topheth, which was in the Valley of Ben Hinnom, so no one could use it to sacrifice their son or daughter in the fire to Molek. He removed from the entrance to the temple of the Lord the horses that the kings of Judah had dedicated to the sun. They were in the court near the room of an official named Nathan-Melek. Josiah then burned the chariots dedicated to the sun.*

*He pulled down the altars the kings of Judah had erected on the roof near the upper room of Ahaz, and the altars Manasseh had built in the two courts of the temple of the Lord. He removed them from there, smashed them to pieces and threw the rubble into the Kidron Valley. The king also desecrated the high places that were east of Jerusalem on the south of the Hill of Corruption—the ones Solomon king of Israel had built for Ashtoreth the vile goddess of the Sidonians, for Chemosh the vile god of Moab, and for Molek the detestable god of the people of Ammon. Josiah smashed the sacred stones and cut down the Asherah poles and covered the sites with human bones.*

The gospel has impacted Europe for over two millennia, going all the way back to the biblical account of Peter on the rooftop of Simon the tanner's home as described in Acts 10. Peter experienced a vision from God of a great sheet coming down from heaven including animals that kosher laws prohibited him from eating. God told him to turn that sheet into a Golden Corral Buffet and eat to his heart's content. Peter argued with God, but the Lord was conveying to him a deeper truth.

Up to this point, the gospel was being proclaimed to none but the Jews only. God was now calling Peter to leave the comfort of his cultural community to take the gospel to the Gentiles as well.

As this vision was occurring God brought men to Peter who represented an Italian Centurion named Cornelius.[38] He, too, was visited with a heavenly vision which needed further explanation. At God's instruction, Cornelius' men set off to find this man named Peter.

God was not only preparing the preacher to preach but the receiver to receive this culture-crossing gospel message. Peter obediently went to preach the gospel to all those gathered at this man's home. As he proclaimed Christ, they all believed, received the baptism of the Holy Spirit, and followed the Lord in water baptism.

From that point on, the full salvation message of the gospel was now being offered to *every tribe, language, people, and nation.*[39] The gospel transformed and impacted cultures so profoundly it resulted in an abandonment of sacred objects in the European civilizations of the day.

As *Boundary Lines* notes;

*When the gospel was originally preached in northern Europe and Britain, the inhabitants of those countries were animists and upon conversion made a complete*

---

[38] A centurion was one of 60 officers in a Roman legion, each of whom commanded 100 men.
[39] Revelation 5:9.

*break with their old animistic worship. Much of their church worship and practice they inherited came from those representatives of the church who brought them the gospel.*[40]

May we never forget Israel's sin of redeeming sacred objects and bringing them into the Temple of God. It is our sin as well when we do the same. This compromise did not result in the blessing of God back then nor does it do so today. The only thing it does is d*rive God far from his sanctuary!*

### Detestable Animals

The prophet was then instructed to dig a hole in the wall of the Temple to find even more detestable things that they were doing. Ezekiel was told;

> *"Son of man, now dig into the wall." So I dug into the wall and saw a doorway there. And he said to me, "Go in and see the wicked and detestable things they are doing here." So I went in and looked, and I saw portrayed all over the walls all kinds of crawling things and unclean animals and all the idols of Israel.*

Israel compromised further by how they chose to decorate the house of God. Plastered over the walls were

---

[40] Ibid, p.17.

these images of *detestable animals* big and small. But that begs the question, *Didn't God make all the animals and call them good?*

The biblical answer is, yes, that is exactly what He did, as recorded in Genesis 1:21-25;

> *So God created the great creatures of the sea and every living thing with which the water teems and that moves about in it, according to their kinds, and every winged bird according to its kind. And God saw that it was good. God blessed them and said, "Be fruitful and increase in number and fill the water in the seas, and let the birds increase on the Earth." And there was evening, and there was morning—the fifth day. And God said, "Let the land produce living creatures according to their kinds: the livestock, the creatures that move along the ground, and the wild animals, each according to its kind." And it was so. God made the wild animals according to their kinds, the livestock according to their kinds, and all the creatures that move along the ground according to their kinds. And God saw that it was good.*

Why does Ezekiel now report God's description of His created animals as *detestable* or *unclean*? Biblical truth articulates that when a people group credit *sacredness* to any animate or inanimate object in their traditional religious system, God is left no option but to change his designation from *good* to *detestably unclean.*

This reality is one of the most critical points in all of Ezekiel's vision and so important to our discussions pertaining to *Indigenous Faith.*

I have heard many times over the years from those in the syncretism camp, *The drum I use is not made by the traditional religion folks. I made it myself (the copied version of the original). That means it no longer is detestable in God's eyes and is something I can now redeem and use for Christian purposes.* When a syncretist comes to your church attempting to bring their sacred objects into the sanctuary of God, the question needs to be asked, *How can you do this when God sees these items as detestable?*

Does it appear to you as it does to me that by making that bold of a statement, the syncretists are putting themselves on a higher plane of understanding than God Himself? Scripture implies it does not matter if a person does not consider an item sacred. What matters to God is when a culture identifies it as such. It is abundantly clear from Ezekiel that God called animals, which He originally created and called good, *detestable,* when nations turned them into their sacred objects.

Moreso, God's second command is to *not make any graven images.* Do not even think about it! The very making of an image that is considered sacred by one's culture is already a violation of that Commandment.

It takes boldness at minimum and arrogance at best to assume we can redeem and call sacred objects good, especially knowing God does not! Again, an honest evaluation of the passage does not leave any wiggle room to squeeze in this kind of unbiblical teaching.

### Strange Smoke

Things do not get any better as Ezekiel continues on his tour of how Israel compromised God's Temple. Ezekiel 8:11-13 says;

*In front of them stood seventy elders of Israel, and Jaazaniah son of Shaphan was standing among them. Each had a censer in his hand, and a fragrant cloud of incense was rising. He said to me, "Son of man, have you seen what the elders of Israel are doing in the darkness, each at the shrine of his own idol? They say, 'The LORD does not see us; the LORD has forsaken the land.'" Again, he said, "You will see them doing things that are even more detestable."*

Generations prior, Moses' *should-have-known-better* nephews, Nadab and Abihu, compromised by using their own unauthorized *fragrant clouds of incense,* which God greatly detested.

These young men were among the most privileged people on earth at the time. They were an integral part of the leadership core of the nation of Israel. God included them as part of the family's *inner core of four*, along with seventy other elders of Israel, who were invited to approach the mountain of God. This would be where God's powerful presence was to be encountered. Exodus 24:1-2 tells us;

*Then the Lord said to Moses, "Come up to the Lord, you and Aaron, Nadab and Abihu, and seventy of the elders of Israel. You are to worship at a distance, but Moses alone is to approach the Lord; the others must not come near. And the people may not come up with him."*

Even though they were considered leaders of Israel and had the favor and blessing of God, they turned away from all that to do something totally against the Holy One of Israel and His clear instruction. They burned the incense not authorized by God (what our tribes call smudging), and it was detestable to God.

Though Scripture is not clear on the exact nature of the offense, in some way they violated God's clear prescription for the offering of incense in Israel's worship of *Yahweh*. They either burned an incense recipe of their own concocting, or syncretized with the incense used by one of the pagan nations around them. Regardless, their act of disobedience brought the ultimate punishment from God as He smote them dead.

The fire that *came out from the presence of the Lord and consumed the burnt offering and the fat portions on the altar,* found in Leviticus 9:24, was the same fire God used to consume these disobedient priests.

Leviticus 10:1-3 says;

> *Aaron's sons Nadab and Abihu took their censers, put fire in them and added incense; and they offered unauthorized fire before the LORD, contrary to his command. So fire came out from the presence of the Lord and consumed them, and they died before the Lord. Moses then said to Aaron, "This is what the Lord spoke of when he said: 'Among those who approach me I will be proved holy; in the sight of all the people I will be honored.' Aaron remained silent.*

Throughout history, there has always been leaders of the House of Israel and leaders of the Body of Christ who have been guilty of doing things their way and in direct opposition to God's commands.

Where did Moses' nephews go wrong in their burning of this incense?

God had prescribed for Israel a unique and very specific recipe for the incense He instructed them to use exclusively for Israel's worship. Exodus 30:34-38, 37:29 tells us;

> *Then the Lord said to Moses, "Take fragrant spices—gum resin, onycha and galbanum—and pure frankincense, all in equal amounts, and make a fragrant blend of incense, the work of a perfumer. It is to be salted and pure and sacred. Grind some of it to powder and place it in front of the ark of the covenant law in the tent of meeting, where I will meet with you. It shall be most holy to you. Do not make any incense with this formula for yourselves; consider it holy to the Lord. Whoever makes incense like it to enjoy its fragrance must be cut off from their people."*
>
> *37:29 They also made the sacred anointing oil and the pure, fragrant incense—the work of a perfumer.*

*Do not make any incense with this formula for yourselves; consider it holy to the Lord,* indicates this was not your everyday incense for personal use. It was to be considered by Israel to be *holy to the Lord.* Israel was bound by the special revelation of God and were not given leeway to bring into the sanctuary of God smoke and incense of other nations around them. That is why God told Ezekiel that these practices were *even more detestable* than the ones already described in the earlier part of Ezekiel's *Tour de Syncretism.*

Incense burning, or smudging, is an important part of the theologies and cultures of indigenous peoples worldwide, including here in North America.

The smudging ceremony is a custom of Native American and other indigenous cultures. For centuries many cultures have used smudging as a way to create a cleansing smoke bath that is used to purify the body, aura, energy, ceremonial/ritual space or any other space and personal articles. Smudging is performed to remove negative energy as well as for centering and healing. Our bodies and environments are not only physical but vibrate with invisible, silent energy.

Smudging calls on the spirits of sacred plants to drive away negative energies and restore balance. Plants such as tobacco, sage, cedar, sweet grass, juniper, lavender and copal are burned and the smoke is directed with a single feather or a fan made of several feathers. Sage is said to purify and drive out negative energy, sweet grass to attract positive energy, beauty and sweetness, cedar to ward off sickness, lavender to bring spiritual blessing. Many tribes consider tobacco to be the most sacred plant, chasing away bad or negative feelings and bringing on good and positive thoughts and to connect people with the spiritual world. Native peoples used tobacco as a medicine, smoked in the evenings and not as a daily occurrence. Tobacco can become a poison when abused and treated without proper respect.

A single plant or mixture of plants is placed in a shell or other fireproof bowl and lit. Some cultures use only shells such as abalone, believing the shell, an element of water, balances the other elements of fire, air, and Earth (plants) while some cultures will not use shells believing that the water element of the shell nullifies the fire element of the smudging. The dried plants are lit and aided in burning by waving a feather, fan or hand. Blowing on the mixture is not advised as it is seen as blowing one's negativity into the mixture as well as blowing away the effectiveness of the plant. The smoke is then wafted around oneself and environment creating a bath of smoke.

Dried plants that are tied into bundles are called smudge sticks, which are lit and burned on one end. Loose plants can be burned in the shell or bowl or placed directly onto burning wood or crumbled over a piece of charcoal.

In native cultures birds are highly revered because of their closeness to Grandfather Creator in the heavens. It is believed the feather possesses the spirit qualities of the bird– to be the breath of life as well as connecting us to the heavens above and mother Earth below. Because of the way they are constructed, it is believed that feathers have the ability to comb someone's energy or aura of blockages therefore aiding in the cleansing smoke bath.

*Indigenous Faith*

> *Ceremonial & dance fans are made by Native Americans from all or part of a wing of an eagle. Some indigenous peoples may use other raptor or exotic bird feathers. Southwestern, Central and South American tribes often use macaw feathers, especially for prayer fans.*[41]

There is spiritual significance to the smudging ceremonies among indigenous tribes. Those who place trust in the power of the smoke and feathers are dependent upon these rituals when faced with challenges, negative issues, or supernatural manifestations.

Tribal gatherings often incorporate smudging ceremonies into their schedules and agendas. Tribal offices often do the same. Native followers of Christ are put in the awkward position of having to decide what they should do as the sacred smoke is coming their way.

What would your choice be, my friend, if faced with this scenario? What does God's Word have to say on the issue? Out of love for Christ, be obedient to what it says.

Galatians 1:10 asks this poignant question;

> *Am I now trying to win the approval of human beings, or of God? Or am I trying to please people? If I were still trying to please people, I would not be a servant of Christ.*

---

[41] http://powwow-power.com/smudging/

Smudging is one of the key elements of indigenous worship offered by the *Redeeming of Culture* movement today. One can now enter some Charismatic, Pentecostal, and even Evangelical churches on many reservations and be met with the aroma of sage, sweetgrass, etc., filling the sanctuary. Compromised worshipers cleanse themselves with the smoke covering their bodies that now serves as a more culturally relevant cleanser. Who then needs the shed blood of Jesus Christ whose blood *cleanses us from all unrighteousness?*[42]

The One and only mediator, Jesus Christ, is minimized and marginalized as a more *culturally appropriate* prayer service is conducted. The smoke attempts to carry the prayers of syncretizers up to the Creator of heaven and earth, not realizing that God has already been *driven far from his sanctuary* and does not allow any *unauthorized fire* to come anywhere near His eternal throne room.

## Unholy Alliances

The prophet is confronted with yet another detestable act of His chosen people. It involved not just the leaders of the house of Israel but now includes their women as well.

Among indigenous people the power and influence of the female cannot be underestimated. Many cultures are

---

[42] 1 John 1:9

matriarchal. The women folk often wield great ceremonial influence and power over their clans and tribes.

The prophet writes in Ezekiel 8:14-15;

*Then he brought me to the entrance of the north gate of the house of the LORD, and I saw women sitting there, mourning the god Tammuz. He said to me, "Do you see this, son of man? You will see things that are even more detestable than this."*

Why such sadness and mourning?

Tammuz was a pagan fertility god of the Babylonians. His influence was so profound that Israel ended up naming the fourth month in their calendar in honor of him. Strong sexual perversion was once again front and center in worship of this god.

His weeping ceremony was connected with agricultural rites. Corn deities were weeping deities who shed fertilizing tears. The sowers simulated the sorrow of divine mourners when they cast seed in the soil to die so that it might spring up as corn. In Egypt the priestesses who acted the parts of Isis and Nepthys, mourned for the slain corn god Osiris, offering themselves in prostitution as a part of their worship.

*Women mourning for Tammuz* was a significant ratcheting up of the syncretistic practices of the children of Israel who joined in at this despicable party. This strong emotional tie, as manifested through the aching hearts of the women of Israel, illustrated that the heart of the people was fully given over to these gods along with their leaders.

We cannot underestimate the damage leaders of compromise bring to those who choose to follow them down roads that lead to destruction. A great accounting awaits leaders who lead people astray. May God help us all!

*Misguided Worship – the Sun*

The final stop on Ezekiel's painful trip ended up just outside the entrance to the Temple where once again, the leaders of the house of Israel brought shame upon themselves and their people.

Ezekiel 8:14-18 says;

*He then brought me into the inner court of the house of the LORD, and there at the entrance to the temple, between the portico and the altar, were about twenty-five men. With their backs toward the temple of the LORD and their faces toward the east, they were bowing down to the sun in the east. He said to me, "Have you seen this, son of man? Is it a trivial matter for the people of Judah to do the detestable things they are doing here? Must they also fill the land with violence and continually arouse my anger? Look at them putting the branch to their nose! Therefore I will deal with them in anger; I will not look on them with pity or spare them. Although they shout in my ears, I will not listen to them."*

Could it get any worse? Twenty-five leaders were caught with their backs toward the temple and worshiping the sun. This needs to be understood literally in order to fully understand the significance of this wicked and detestable action.

In order to be a syncretizer, one must literally turn their back on God's Word. Israel did, and the results were devastating as they once again chose error over truth. God had already given them clear instructions on the items that Ezekiel saw in this vision, as recorded in the book of Deuteronomy 4:15-20;

*You saw no form of any kind the day the Lord spoke to you at Horeb out of the fire. Therefore watch yourselves very carefully, so that you do not become corrupt and make for yourselves an idol, an image of any shape, whether formed like a man or a woman or like any animal on Earth or any bird that flies in the air, or like any creature that moves along the ground or any fish in the waters below. And when you look up to the sky and see the sun, the moon and the stars—all the heavenly array—do not be enticed into bowing down to them and worshiping things the Lord your God has apportioned to all the nations under heaven. But as for you, the Lord took you and brought you out of the iron-smelting furnace, out of Egypt, to be the people of his inheritance, as you now are.*

Ezekiel saw these particular leaders *bowing down to the sun in the east.*

Sun worship originated with the Babylonians, Persians, and Egyptians. It eventually was embraced by the Greeks and Romans and indigenous people worldwide, including those on the North American continent. It is still practiced among some of our Native American tribes today.

The blood of sun worshipers is shed in these ceremonies for the remission of sins. While this form of worship is connected with indigenous people worldwide, it stands in total contradiction to the clear gospel message of *grace alone through faith alone in Christ alone.*

## Israel's Reason, God's Response

In Ezekiel's documentation of Israel's syncretistic behavior we are not left wondering why they did what they did. Their rationale is included by God in His Word for all to see.

Ezekiel 8:12 states;

*The Lord does not see us; the Lord has forsaken the land.*

This is the same rationale the *Redeeming of Culture movement* uses today as they seek to defend their reactionary compromises. They believe that God is not seeing and responding to the needs evident in Native North America due to the myriad of mistakes made in historical missionary efforts.

My assessment is; they believe that missiological strategy needs to be overhauled based on an assumption that, *If only we could make Jesus look more Native, then our people would respond in greater numbers to His message of salvation.*

We cannot leave Ezekiel's amazing vision without a reminder of God's reaction. How did the Creator of heaven and earth respond to Israel's collusion with Satan?

Ezekiel 8:6 says;

*Son of man, do you see what they are doing—the utterly detestable things the Israelites are doing here, things that will drive me far from my sanctuary?*

Ezekiel 8:18 emphatically states;

*Therefore I will deal with them in anger; I will not look on them with pity or spare them. Although they shout in my ears, I will not listen to them.*

God does not come down to visit and bless syncretistic behavior. It matters not if a syncretist believes he is actually serving God and His purposes. God turns a deaf ear to not only their cries and prayers, but to those they mislead.

At this point, I need to answer a very important question that no doubt arises in some minds. *Are you saying, Craig, that a syncretist is not saved or beyond redemption? Which camp are they in, Satan's or God's?*

Only Sovereign God knows whose names are written in what the Scriptures call *the Lamb's Book of Life*. He does give us assurance of our salvation when we come to Him through saving faith in Jesus Christ. Along with scriptural passages that call us to repentance for the forgiveness of sin,

1 John 5:13 says;

*I write these things to you who believe in the name of the Son of God so that you may know that you have eternal life.*

It is also true that some who believe they are saved actually are not!

Matthew 7:21-23 says;

*Not everyone who says to me, 'Lord, Lord,' will enter the kingdom of heaven, but only the one who does the will of my Father who is in heaven. Many will say to me on that day, 'Lord, Lord, did we not prophesy in your name and in your name drive out demons and in your name perform many miracles?' Then I will tell them plainly, 'I never knew you. Away from me, you evildoers!'*

The bottom line is, when Israel and its leaders obeyed God's Word, they were blessed. When they disobeyed they suffered His wrath.

Scripture also affirms the reality that some leaders have been carried about with an unholy *duplicity of allegiance*. They were busy bowing one knee to God while at the same time bowing the other knee to the gods of this world.

Zephaniah 1:4-6 says;

*I will stretch out my hand against Judah and against all who live in Jerusalem. I will destroy every remnant of Baal worship in this place, the very names of the idolatrous priests— those who bow down on the roofs to worship the starry host, those who bow down and swear by the Lord and who also swear by Molek, those who turn back from following the Lord and neither seek the Lord nor inquire of him.*

That is blatant disobedience for sure, my friend. It should be grievous to our hearts, whether we read about it back in Zephaniah's day, or see it with our own eyes among the false teachers of our day.

As I close this chapter, I invite you to ponder what A.W. Tozer so famously said;

*Grace will save a man...but it will not save him and his idol.*

*Chapter Eight*

# THE "COME DOWN" KINGDOM

**THROUGHOUT HUMAN HISTORY NATIONS HAVE RISEN** and fallen. Due to the ingrained pride in all of us, wars and rumors of wars among tribes, nations, and people groups have continued unabated, since we were all shooed off the plains of Shinar.

Scripture is clear that cultures, world religions, and worldviews have developed within the context of fallen humanity. In the midst of the chaos, and in the fullness of time, God chose to come down from on high, and introduce a heaven-sent remedy for the malady of all nations. It is His redemptive plan that features the second member of the Trinity, God the Son, Jesus the Christ, the Savior of all the world.

It is important to realize that everything about Christ, His redemptive plan, His Church, and His Kingdom have come to us from another place...*a higher place*. It is completely distinct and different from anything ever experienced by the inhabitants of Planet Earth! It is a come down thing! It is a COME DOWN KINGDOM!

We have already seen in the Old Testament where God *came down* to earth at various times such as His visit to the plains of Shinar in Genesis 11. That is not the only time God had to *come down* to make a statement to the people that He created.

There was another *Christophany* (a manifestation on earth of the pre-incarnate Christ) that occurred as Israel, under the guidance of Joshua, made their way into the Promised Land. Joshua records this important encounter with the pre-incarnate King of kings in Joshua 5:13-16;

> *Now when Joshua was near Jericho, he looked up and saw a man standing in front of him with a drawn sword in his hand. Joshua went up to him and asked, "Are you for us or for our enemies?" "Neither," he replied, "but as commander of the army of the Lord I have now come." Then Joshua fell facedown to the ground in reverence, and asked him, "What message does my Lord have for his servant?" The commander of the Lord's army replied, "Take off your sandals, for the place where you are standing is holy." And Joshua did so.*

Anytime God chose to *come down* to His creation signified a very important lesson, not only for Israel but also for the rest of us.

The image Joshua had was of a man *standing in front of him with a drawn sword in his hand.* He inquired as to whose side this man was on. A*re you for us or for our enemies?*

This *Come Down Creator* emphatically answers, *Neither!*

His alignment with Israel was contingent on them walking in obedience! That is the side He has always been committed to, my friend. Being His chosen people did not exempt them from obedience. It only made it that much more important. If they did so, it would keep the *commander of the Lord's army* on their side.

What was the issue that made God so tentative in His commitment to being on their side? It is recorded for us in Joshua 6:17-19;

*The city and all that is in it are to be devoted to the Lord. Only Rahab the prostitute and all who are with her in her house shall be spared, because she hid the spies we sent. But keep away from the devoted things, so that you will not bring about your own destruction by taking any of them. Otherwise you will make the camp of Israel liable to destruction and bring trouble on it. All the silver and gold and the articles of bronze and iron are sacred to the Lord and must go into his treasury.*

It is important to not get confused when looking at this passage. Some may want to argue that Scripture is speaking out of both sides of its mouth, as it first says everything in the city is to be *devoted to the Lord* before it instructs Israel to keep away from the *devoted things*. One would be tempted to argue that God accepts the devoted things of the nations, so we should not be so opposed to redeeming sacred objects.

The clarifier is found in verse 19 where it states;

*All the silver and gold and the articles of bronze and iron are sacred to the Lord and must go into his treasury.*

To understand this passage, we must recognize there are two kinds of *devoted things* being identified by the *Captain of the Lord's Army*.

First, there were *devoted things of the nations* (the sacred objects) that were now to be given over to the Lord *for the purpose of destruction*. That has always been the Lord's position on any sacred objects of any nation. It was those things Israel was commanded to keep away from.

There was a second group of *devoted things* that God kept for Himself. He gave Israel permission to collect and keep the spoils of victory, such as *all the silver, gold, and articles of bronze*. These were assets to be deposited into the Lord's treasury for the purpose of providing for the ongoing costs of keeping the lights on.

This *Come Down Kingdom* is clearly seen throughout the pages of revealed Scripture. It serves as great encouragement to the current band of believers who are just passing through this life to a better land and a better place, *whose builder and maker is God* (Hebrews 11:10b).

It is an eternal Kingdom, but one we do not have to wait for. It is a Kingdom that has *come down* to us when God sent His Son over two thousand years ago. He opened the entrance gate of this Kingdom to all who would be saved through Jesus Christ our Lord.

To get to those gates, walk with me first through the Garden of Gethsemane. It was there in deep anguish God's beloved Son wrestled with His own humanity.

Matthew 26:38-39 says;

*Then he said to them, "My soul is overwhelmed with sorrow to the point of death. Stay here and keep watch with me." Going a little farther, he fell with his face to the ground and prayed, "My Father, if it is possible, may this cup be taken from me. Yet not as I will, but as you will."*

God, Himself, took on human flesh, emotions, and reactions just like the rest of us. He had to fight the humanly appropriate reaction of not wanting to go through such pain and suffering.

Thankfully, His Deity was also there in Gethsemane's garden reminding His humanity that before time began this was to be the only Way of redemption for lost mankind. He came through the ordeal fully committed to the suffering awaiting Him up Calvary's hill.

From the garden of anguish, we follow His footsteps up the dusty road leading to Calvary's mount and arrive at the place where the cross that Jesus Christ was nailed on was lowered into the ground.

I now must leave you in front of the cross to make your decision about what you are going to do with this Savior and the sacrifice He made on your behalf. It is here where you are left with only one of two options. You must choose to align yourself with one of the two thieves who were hanging on either side of Jesus.

These two criminals represent all mankind. On one side is an unrepentant mocker who chose to reject Christ and His atoning sacrifice.

Luke 23:39 reminds us;

*One of the criminals who hung there hurled insults at him: "Aren't you the Christ? Save yourself and us!"*

On the other side is the repentant thief who reminded the other that they should be the only two that day to hang on their crosses and pay for their crimes.

Luke 23:40 says;

*"Don't you fear God," he said, "since you are under the same sentence? We are punished justly, for we are getting what our deeds deserve. But this man has done nothing wrong."*

He then turns to Christ seeking mercy and forgiveness. Luke 23:42 says;

*Jesus, remember me when you come into your kingdom.*

The side you choose will determine your eternal destiny.

Pass by it on the side of the ridiculing unrepentant thief and you are choosing to be counted with all those who reject Christ, His forgiveness, and gift of eternal life.

Pass by it on the side of the repentant thief who cried out to Jesus for forgiveness with a broken and contrite heart, and you, too, will receive Christ's gift of eternal life.

The repentant thief understood enough to know there was a Kingdom that was associated with Christ, and it was yet to come. What he didn't realize is he would become the very first person in human history that would enter that Kingdom through Christ's suffering and atoning death.

Jesus affirms the reality that the Kingdom of God had already come to earth. His comforting reply to this guilty thief still shocks the skeptics and arrogant to this day. He said to him, as recorded in Luke 23:43;

*I tell you the truth, today you will be with me in paradise.*

That day only one guilty thief out of two entered into the Kingdom of God!

Since then, we all must pass by the empty tomb as well. You won't find Him, though. He no longer is there! He is alive forever more!

John 11:25-27 says;

*"I am the resurrection and the life. The one who believes in me will live, even though they die; and whoever lives by believing in me will never die. Do you believe this?" "Yes, Lord," she replied, "I believe that you are the Messiah, the Son of God, who is to come into the world."*

Believing in the death, burial, and resurrection of Jesus Christ puts the keys to the Kingdom of God in your hands. Transferring your complete trust into Jesus Christ's salvation plan inserts the key into the lock and opens the only door into His eternal Kingdom.

This *Come Down Kingdom* also has its own *Come Down Messenger*.

Galatians 4:4-5 tells us;

*But when the set time had fully come, God sent his Son, born of a woman, born under the law, to redeem those under the law, that we might receive adoption to sonship.*

Scripture tells us that His throne room is in heaven, and the earth is His footstool.

As Isaiah 66:1 notes;

*This is what the Lord says: "Heaven is my throne, and the earth is my footstool."*

The universe is too small to contain Him, yet He inhabits the hearts and minds of those who are His! The old gospel song says it right, *He left the splendor of heaven, knowing His destiny, 'twas the lonely hill of Golgatha, there to lay down His life for me.*[43]

The *Come Down Messenger* had to journey from heaven to earth for God's salvation plan to be completed. This makes the gospel and Christ's message unique from all world religions birthed out of fallen human cultures.

This *Come Down Kingdom* also includes a *Come Down Church*.

Hebrews 12:23 states;

*...to the church of the firstborn, whose names are written in heaven...*

So, what is the church? It is definitely not a building. It is the people of God who Christ gave His life for. They assemble themselves under the banner of the cross to sing and praise God as they grow closer to God and each other. They are

---
[43] *If That Isn't Love,* by Dottie Rambo

led by an anointed pastor who shepherds them by taking them to feed regularly on God's Holy Word. God's Holy Spirit helps them discover ways of serving the Lord and others with their spiritual gifts and callings. This should be the goal every indigenous church strives for.

Devoted followers of Christ implement what they have learned by living a godly life at home and in the community. They can't keep the gospel to themselves! They want to share it with their community and do so by proclaiming the gospel. That is the real Church the Scriptures identify as authentic and representative of the Kingdom of God.

One could ask a church for their membership list to see who they all are. In doing so, however, we must not forget what the writer of Hebrews said when he identified where the real membership rolls of Christ's Church are recorded - *the church of the firstborn, whose names are written in heaven.*

Scripture tells us the only record keeping of the Church that really matters is not here on earth, but in heaven! Tell me, what other human institution has heaven for its international office? The real headquarters of the Church of the Living God is not to be found near some access ramp off a local freeway. That sweet lady's voice in your car's GPS system will never be able to pinpoint the Church's main office address, my friend! You have to look to a higher place, up yonder in heaven, to find the true registration book of those who are citizens of the Kingdom of God!

We are also the *church of the firstborn.*

Colossians 1:18 tells us; *And he is the head of the body, the church; he is the beginning and the firstborn from among the dead, so that in everything he might have the supremacy.*

Not only is the headquarters of the church today in heaven, but so is the King who presides over this blood bought band of believers. The Senior Pastor of the true Church of God is, right now, *seated at the right hand of the Father, making intercession for us* (Colossians 3:1)!

The church existing around the world today is directly tied to a place so far away but yet so near to each of us. Heaven is a reality, and it is the current and future home of the *church of the firstborn, whose names are written in heaven.*

In God's great design, the Church of the Living God is a *Come Down Church*!

Everything about God's Kingdom is summarized in this reality. It is a *Come Down Kingdom.*

Mark 1:15 states;

*"The time has come," he said. "The kingdom of God has come near. Repent and believe the good news!"*

It is hard for Americans to understand the nature and workings of a kingdom, because we as a nation have always been a *Constitutional Republic*. Government of the people, by the people, and for the people, has defined the larger American society since the Declaration of Independence. If you don't like the rulers we elect, in the next election cycle we are free to throw the bums out! Not so in a kingdom, though.

A kingdom has *a King.* That King has absolute sovereignty over his subjects and rules with complete authority. A monarchy replaces a democracy, which is two completely separate ways of governing people.

The King of this Kingdom is none other than Jesus Christ! He rules and reigns over this Kingdom, and does so with sovereign authority. As members of His Kingdom, we are His subjects, graciously and lovingly bowing down before Him as we offer Him our ongoing praise and adoration. We are called to serve Him and to lovingly obey His orders.

No servant dictates to the king rules and regulations he desires to live by. It is always the other way around. The King of this Kingdom doesn't rule as a tyrant or with an iron fist. He calls his subjects *His own.* His orders are love based and motivated.

This King sacrificed it all to open the door for those who respond to His invitation to be a part of this Kingdom. Only tyrannical kings would sacrifice their subjects to further their rule and reign. Not this King!

## The "Come Down" Kingdom

Pondering these realities brings me willingly down on my knees in humble submission to Him. What He calls me to do, I do with gratitude in my heart, even if it involves suffering and pain. In doing so, more honor and glory goes to Him as my King and not to me as His subject. That is what living in the Kingdom of God is all about.

It is so important to remember that all this came at such a high price (Ephesians 2:11-22).

*Therefore, remember that formerly you who are Gentiles by birth and called "uncircumcised" by those who call themselves "the circumcision" (which is done in the body by human hands)— remember that at that time you were separate from Christ, excluded from citizenship in Israel and foreigners to the covenants of the promise, without hope and without God in the world. But now in Christ Jesus you who once were far away have been brought near by the blood of Christ. For he himself is our peace, who has made the two groups one and has destroyed the barrier, the dividing wall of hostility, by setting aside in his flesh the law with its commands and regulations. His purpose was to create in himself one new humanity out of the two, thus making peace, and in one body to reconcile both of them to God through the cross, by which he put to death their hostility. He came and preached peace to you who were far away and peace to those who were near. For through him we both have access to the Father by one Spirit. Consequently, you are no longer foreigners and strangers, but fellow citizens with God's people and also members of his household, built on the foundation of the apostles and prophets, with Christ Jesus himself as the chief cornerstone. In him the whole building is joined together and rises to become a holy temple in the Lord. And in him you too are being built together to become a dwelling in which God lives by his Spirit.*

### Living as People of the Kingdom of God

God saves people from all nations who respond to the gospel's exclusive message. Scripture says He calls out for Himself those *from every tribe, language, people, and nation* (Revelation 7:9).

*Biblical redemption* is strictly *vertical* but *biblical reconciliation* is both *vertical* and *horizontal*. I become not only reconciled to God, but to all others with whom I may even have historically harbored anger and resentment against. That is true biblical reconciliation!

Kingdom people do not move from one sin-stained culture to another. We move up to a higher level of living as mutual members of the Kingdom of God. Believers from every tribe, language, people, and nation now mutually possess a biblically defined identity and culture as we love Christ and obey His Holy Word.

That does not mean I lose all my earthly culture and identity. However, I must now render those things subordinate to the biblical truth that governs the Kingdom of God. There are many things in human cultures that do not violate God's standards. We can celebrate and incorporate those things that conform to the standards of God's Word.

In some remote village eight thousand miles away, another indigenous person comes to saving faith in Jesus Christ. He and I now have become part of the same Kingdom of God. We have now become brothers in Christ.

While our human cultures may be totally different, our new life in Christ now displays important similarities, because we both are reading and applying God's instruction Book on holy living. It will be especially evident when we are obediently abandoning the usage of any sacred objects of our past. Why? Because God's Word instructs us both to do so if we are to live lives pleasing to God.

As we mature in our faith we long to do things that please God, while our love for the Savior grows deeper in our hearts. Our love for each other as members of the same family does as well. That is one of the great blessings of living in this *Come Down Kingdom*!

It is easy to not have contempt or anger between me and a brother when eight thousand miles separates us. It is because we have not had to interact, in our old life, with his culture or nation. Isolation helps keep the peace. What happens though, when someone from the culture right next door becomes a part of the Kingdom of God? What if there has been hatred and hostility harbored between us in the past? How do we reconcile past hostility with current biblical reality in this *Come Down Kingdom?*

Ephesians 2 is so important for understanding Kingdom living. Remember what Paul said in verse 13?

*But now in Christ Jesus you who once were far away have been brought near by the blood of Christ.*

This isn't a PC issue (political correctness), it is a BC issue (blood of Christ)! Kingdom living means I accept the uncomfortable reality that just as much blood of Jesus was shed to reconcile us *horizontally to each other* as to reconcile us *vertically to God*! That is huge as we seek to live lives that honor the Lord and honor the sacrifice He made on our behalf.

Crucial to living as Kingdom people is to love, cherish, and interact with fellow believers in Christ from all other cultures. The shed blood of Christ was meant to build bridges, not barriers, between those who *were sometimes afar off.*

I now have more in common with a believer in Jesus Christ in a faraway land or even just across the street, than I do with those from within my own community or culture who choose not to follow Christ. *Biblical identity and significance* must take precedence over *cultural identity and significance.* Doing so enables us to experience the full impact of what living in the Kingdom of God offers.

*Our Identity and Significance*

The Apostle Paul helps the believer in the area of our new identity and significance as he writes in Philippians 3:4-11;

*...If someone else thinks they have reasons to put confidence in the flesh, I have more: circumcised on the eighth day, of the people of Israel, of the tribe of Benjamin, a Hebrew of Hebrews; in regard to the law, a Pharisee; as for zeal, persecuting the church; as for righteousness based on the law, faultless. But whatever were gains to me I now consider loss for the sake of Christ. What is more, I consider everything a loss because of the surpassing worth of knowing Christ Jesus my Lord, for whose sake I have lost all things. I consider them garbage, that I may gain Christ and be found in him, not having a righteousness of my own that comes from the law, but that which is through faith in Christ—the righteousness that comes from God on the basis of faith. I want to know Christ—yes, to know the power of his resurrection and participation in his sufferings, becoming like him in his death, and so, somehow, attaining to the resurrection from the dead.*

This was an amazing statement coming from a man who, before coming to Christ, was one of his chief adversaries. He hated Christ and Christianity. He had believers arrested, tortured, and imprisoned, while others he made pay the ultimate price through martyrdom.

This man's torturous career begins in Acts 7. Saul (who later became the Apostle Paul) was there consenting to the death of an early layman in the Church named Stephen. This bold believer in Christ was sharing with the Jewish leaders a convicting history lesson of Israel's waywardness. The whole chapter is an important read. It leads to Israel's crucifixion of Christ and the rejection of His salvation message.

Stephen summarizes his powerful sermon in Acts 7:51-53;

> *"You stiff-necked people! Your hearts and ears are still uncircumcised. You are just like your ancestors: You always resist the Holy Spirit! Was there ever a prophet your ancestors did not persecute? They even killed those who predicted the coming of the Righteous One. And now you have betrayed and murdered him—you who have received the law that was given through angels but have not obeyed it."*

Saul's deep involvement in this sordid act of mob violence is recorded for us in Acts 7:54-60;

> *When the members of the Sanhedrin heard this, they were furious and gnashed their teeth at him. But Stephen, full of the Holy Spirit, looked up to heaven and saw the glory of God, and Jesus standing at the right hand of God. "Look," he said, "I see heaven open and the Son of Man standing at the right hand of God." At this they covered their ears and, yelling at the top of their voices, they all rushed at him, dragged him out of the city and began to stone him. Meanwhile, the witnesses laid their coats at the feet of a young man named Saul. While they were stoning him, Stephen prayed, "Lord Jesus, receive my spirit." Then he fell on his knees and cried out, "Lord, do not hold this sin against them." When he had said this, he fell asleep.*

Later on, while traveling on the road to Damascus, Saul is miraculously saved and becomes a committed follower of Christ. He now considers the earthly vestiges of his old identity and significance as non-essential when compared to the *surpassing greatness of knowing Christ.*

This passage reveals very important truths about Paul. First, we find out that he was a *tribal man.*

Verse 5 tells us;

> *circumcised on the eighth day, of the people of Israel, of the tribe of Benjamin...*

His ancestry links him to the tribe of Benjamin, who was the twelfth and final son of Jacob. Each of Jacob's sons were the progenitors of the twelve tribes of Israel. In offering his prophetic blessings on his twelve sons, Jacob blesses his youngest with the following blessing, as recorded in Genesis 49:27;

*Benjamin is a ravenous wolf; in the morning he shall devour the prey, and at night he shall divide the spoil.*

Scripture identifies four prominent figures from the tribe of Benjamin, three from the Old Testament, and one from the New Testament.

First was Ehud, a great warrior who delivered Israel from the Moabites (Judges 3:12-30). Next was Saul, who becomes the first king of Israel (1 Samuel 9:15-27). In later Jewish history, while many Jews were living in Persia, God used Mordecai and Esther, from the tribe of Benjamin, to deliver the Jews from death (Esther 2:5-7). Finally, in the New Testament the Apostle Paul affirms he, too, came from the lineage of Benjamin.

Is it any wonder that Saul, while living under the Benjamite mantle before coming to Christ, was such a violent and ravenous wolf when it came to persecuting the church? To put it in the modern vernacular, *That's how we Benjamites roll, homey!*

What are the hallmarks and reputation of your family lineage in your community? What are you and your *homeys* known for? For Paul, he was perfectly aligned with the image his tribe was known for. He was the poster child for the tribe of Benjamin! But again, that was before he came to Christ. Things change, and change dramatically, as we will soon see, when a person's identity and significance is transferred to Christ!

He was not only a *tribal man*, he was also a *linguistic man*, as verse 5 continues;

*a Hebrew of Hebrews...*

Since Shinar's plains, languages have become so important to the life of a tribe or people. If you know the language you're someone special. If not, you are made to feel that something very important is missing. Paul's identity and significance was attached in a huge way to his ability to communicate in the language of his people. As far as Paul was concerned, there was no doubt he was highly respected and revered because linguistically, he was *the man!*

This leads to the next identifier.

He was not only a *tribal* and *linguistic man,* he was a *traditional* man. Verse 5 says;

*in regard to the law, a Pharisee...*

## Indigenous Faith

A historian named Josephus, who lived around the time of Christ, defined the Pharisees as those who;

*follow the guidance of that which their doctrine has selected and transmitted as good, attaching the chief importance to the observance of those commandments which it has seen fit to dictate to them.*[44]

Jesus had much to say about the Pharisees, because He knew that, while they were committed to the traditions of their forefathers, they were more concerned about the keeping of the rules and regulations while their hearts (motives and intent), were far removed from those laws.

Late author and speaker, Dr. Jerry Bridges notes;

*The most proximate cause of the Pharisees' antagonism toward Jesus, however, lay in His ignoring of their hundreds of elaborate but petty rules that they had devised for interpreting the law of God. Not only did they devise these hundreds of man-made rules, but they had also elevated them to the level of Scripture, so that to break one of their rules was to violate the law of God itself. And yet these rules not only obscured the true intent of God's law, but also, in some cases, actually violated it, as stated in Mark 7:9-13;*

---

[44] http://www.biblestudytools.com/dictionary/pharisees/

> *And he said to them, "You have a fine way of rejecting the commandment of God in order to establish your tradition! For Moses said, 'Honor your father and your mother'; and, 'Whoever reviles father or mother must surely die.' But you say, 'If a man tells his father or his mother, "Whatever you would have gained from me is Corban" (that is, devoted to God)* — *then you no longer permit him to do anything for his father or mother, thus making void the word of God by your tradition that you have handed down. And many such things you do."*[45]

*Corban* was a term that described something Israel had dedicated to God and could no longer be used in the typical way. In this case, some in Israel excused themselves from taking care of their elderly parents by saying that the time and resources needed to do so was *Corban*, or, dedicated over to God.

They could not fulfill this basic responsibility, because their tradition offered them an off ramp from the freeway of faithfulness in this important family responsibility. That's how low Israel had stooped in their pursuit of tradition. Just call it *Corban* whenever you don't want to do it and are looking for some *spiritual excuse* to cover *ungodly* attitudes and actions.

Like Paul, you can be a traditional person and yet miss the real point of life. Keeping tradition for tradition's sake

---

[45] http://www.ligonier.org/learn/articles/jesus-challenges-pharisees/

will never satisfy the deep longings of the heart. In the hot pursuit of tradition one can manage to ice the heart and redirect its affection to lesser things.

Is there room in your heart to ask, *God, have I been wrong all along? Is the Word of God really true? Have I missed the purpose of life while trying to find identity and significance in things other than You?*

Misguided affections and allegiances can eventually lead to hostile behavior. It did to Paul. Just look at Paul again, before coming to Christ. He became a *militant man!*

Verse 6 continues;

*as for zeal, persecuting the church...*

The ravenous wolf of Genesis 49 was alive and well in the life of this persecutor turned preacher. On his trip to Damascus he encountered Christ in a profound way! This incredible occurrence happened after Jesus' ascension to heaven.

Acts 9:1-17 says;

*Meanwhile, Saul was still breathing out murderous threats against the Lord's disciples. He went to the high priest and asked him for letters to the synagogues in Damascus, so that if he found any there who belonged to the Way, whether men or women, he might take them as prisoners to Jerusalem. As he neared Damascus on his* journey, suddenly a light from heaven flashed around him. He fell to the ground and heard a voice say to him, "Saul, Saul, why do you persecute me?"

"Who are you, Lord?" Saul asked. "I am Jesus, whom you are persecuting," he replied. "Now get up and go into the city, and you will be told what you must do."

The men traveling with Saul stood there speechless; they heard the sound but did not see anyone. Saul got up from the ground, but when he opened his eyes he could see nothing. So they led him by the hand into Damascus. For three days he was blind, and did not eat or drink anything.

In Damascus there was a disciple named Ananias. The Lord called to him in a vision, "Ananias!" "Yes, Lord," he answered. The Lord told him, "Go to the house of Judas on Straight Street and ask for a man from Tarsus named Saul, for he is praying. In a vision he has seen a man named Ananias come and place his hands on him to restore his sight."

"Lord," Ananias answered, "I have heard many reports about this man and all the harm he has done to your holy people in Jerusalem. And he has come here with authority from the chief priests to arrest all who call on your name." But the Lord said to Ananias, "Go! This man is my chosen *instrument to proclaim my name to the Gentiles and their kings and to the people of Israel. I will show him how much he must suffer for my name."*

The Damascus journey was not a vacation getaway for Saul. It was a business trip. His business was the collecting, imprisoning, and punishing of God's people. You can't get more militant than that.

Our hearts sink when the news reporters tell of another group of Christians who have just been beheaded at the hand of militant groups filled with hatred and disdain for God and His people. Ravenous wolves still exist, and rise up again and again to persecute God's chosen and redeemed people.

Within our indigenous communities most people understand not all tribal members choose to be *Tradish*, but instead choose to follow other ways, including Christianity. And that's ok with them. Many of our neighbors and friends are just that – good neighbors and close friends. By and large, there is mutual respect within the community.

Sometimes there are those within a community who choose to take a more militant position that express itself through verbal attacks, shunning, speaking falsely, and other forms of shaming those who stray from the traditional way.

In some communities, tradition's fervor can and has led to the carrying out of physical or property harm to a Christ follower. Paul was that kind of guy. He hated Christ and he hated Christians. He wasn't slack in allowing that zeal to call on his darker side.

Finally, Paul's letter to the Philippians indicated that he was also a very *religious man*!

Philippians 4:6 concludes;

*...as for righteousness based on the law, faultless.*

His passionate pursuit of Judaism before following Christ reminds us that it is possible to be very religious, and yet miss true religion, which is found only in Christ and in a personal relationship with Him.

Because Paul was a man formerly steeped in the religion of his ancestors, he played an important role in helping his people understand the difference between Christianity and Judaism. He could speak to the issues with great authority and understanding, because he knew the intricacies at play. We can learn much from Paul's words to the Philippians. They are very significant and relevant to us as we live out *Indigenous Faith.*

These identifiers gave the pre-Christian Paul his identity and significance. Now as a follower of Christ his identity and significance no long rests in his culture, traditions, or old religion.

He articulates what true transformation looks like in the life of the *worst among sinners.*

1 Tim. 1:15 describes Paul in this way;

*Here is a trustworthy saying that deserves full acceptance: Christ Jesus came into the world to save sinners—of whom I am the worst.*

He goes on to say in Philippians 3:7-11;

*But whatever were gains to me I now consider loss for the sake of Christ. What is more, I consider everything a loss because of the surpassing worth of knowing Christ Jesus my Lord, for whose sake I have lost all things. I consider them garbage, that I may gain Christ and be found in him, not having a righteousness of my own that comes from the law, but that which is through faith in Christ—the righteousness that comes from God on the basis of faith. I want to know Christ—yes, to know the power of his resurrection and participation in his sufferings, becoming like him in his death, and so, somehow, attaining to the resurrection from the dead...*

Can we say the same about how we view our own attachments to our human cultures and traditions? This is pretty heavy stuff my friend, and a crucial place to come to if we are to experience the full life in Christ and go deeper in Him than we ever thought we could!

From my own experience, I've concluded that culture and traditions can only do so much, and only go so far, especially when lined up side by side to the power of the indwelling Christ!

- Culture can lead you, but it can never love you...
- Culture can influence you, but it can never indwell you...
- Culture can guide you, but it can never guard you...
- Traditions can teach you, but they can never transform you...
- Traditions can direct you, but they can never protect you...
- Culture can esteem you, but it can never redeem you...
- Culture can inform you, but it can never transform you...
- Culture can guide you on earth, but it can never get you into heaven...
- Tradition can show you how to live, but it can never show you how to die...
- Culture can show you how to cope, but can never give you lasting hope...
- Culture can influence your years, but it can never calm your fears, let alone dry your tears.

These lessons were burned into my heart while going through the greatest physical challenge of my life. I had just passed through death's door in a Santa Fe, New Mexico emergency room. For weeks on end, I laid comatose and clinging to life in a Trauma Center ICU unit in Albuquerque, New Mexico.

> Yes, I can attest, as the apostle Paul noted, there is a *surpassing worth of knowing Christ Jesus my Lord, for whose sake I have lost all things. I consider them garbage, that I may gain Christ and be found in him, not having a righteousness of my own that comes from the law, but that which is through faith in Christ—the righteousness that comes from God on the basis of faith.*

### Haman, Xerxes and God's People

Back in the Old Testament a Jew hater named Haman was complaining to the ruler of the Medes and Persians, King Xerxes, about God's covenant people, Israel. He wanted to have them all killed. He said this about them, as recorded in Esther 4:8;

> *There is a certain people dispersed among the peoples in all the provinces of your kingdom who keep themselves separate. Their customs are different from those of all other people, and they do not obey the king's laws; it is not in the king's best interest to tolerate them.*

That has always been the mark of the people of God. We do not live according to the customs and traditions of any human culture we've been redeemed from. We are to live our lives so in line with God's Word, because we are so in love with God's Son, people will look at us and say, these folks live differently from the rest of us!

We do not need Jesus to look more *indigenous.* What is needed is *indigenous people* looking more and more like Jesus!

# PART 3
# DEVELOPING
# THE STRATEGY

*Chapter Nine*

# WHAT TO SURRENDER, WHAT TO KEEP

WE'VE COVERED A LOT OF TERRITORY SO FAR, BUT THERE are still important issues that need to be addressed. We must now put feet to the biblical foundation on how to live God honoring *Indigenous Faith*. It is not by mistake that two of the three sections focus on building a theological foundation. Any pursuit of the practical without such can lead any one of us to the same conclusions that have plagued those who succumb to syncretistic practices.

God's Word is clear that our sacred objects are to be abandoned, destroyed, and distanced from us if we are to live out healthy *Indigenous Faith.* There is more to our culture than just sacred objects, though. Every culture possesses *cultural forms* and *meanings* that guide them in ways that are normative. Sorting out what cultural forms and meanings we can keep, which ones must be changed or, even abandoned, is done through *critical contextualization*.

This process begins before a culture has been exposed to the gospel by missionaries who attempt to bridge the cultural divides and share the gospel. It finds its best days when local believers, who know the culture best, grow in knowledge of God's Word and continue refining the contextualization process.

This is what Christian higher education appropriately teaches those going into cross-cultural ministry. It is an important part of missionary training that we stand one-hundred percent behind. We do so only if the professors do not include what the *Redeeming of Culture* movement promotes.

The *Redeeming of Culture* movement self-identifies as those who, after five-hundred years of mistakes, are the *real contextualizers* who are finally doing it right. Academia has embraced this movement without knowing the full story of what is attempting to be redeemed.

How will academia react to these truths? Does a high view commitment to the authority of Scripture even remain in Christian higher education?

My heartfelt plea to the Christian academic world is, *Do not listen to what the syncretizers or even what I have to say on these matters.* In the end none of our words really matter. What really matters is *what does God's Word have to say*? Go back to its pages and confirm what is truth. In the end that is all that matters!

Native Evangelical leaders committed to the authority of Scripture will be watching with great interest to see how our educators respond, especially after this important delineation between culture and sacred objects is considered.

What then are the things we can keep? How do we live for Jesus while still living surrounded by our traditional cultures and religions?

*Getting Practical on What to Surrender, What to Keep*

While our sacred objects are to be abandoned, the other parts of our culture need to be evaluated through the theological grid of the *Kingdom of God*. True *Indigenous Faith* differentiates between our sacred objects and cultural forms and meanings.

In order to process culture, it is crucial to ask, *What is the definition we are all working from?*

The C&MA's Native Theological Task Force definition is plain, simple, and historically endorsed. It is the one I present to you for your consideration.

*Boundary Lines* states;

Culture:

*The civilization of a given people, nation at a given time, or over all time; its customs, its arts, its conveniences.* [46]

What are a culture's *customs, arts and conveniences*?

We define customs to mean;

---

[46] Ibid. Page 31

> *Any usual action or practice; habit; the accepted way of acting in a community or other group; tradition; or a long-established habit that has almost the force of law. An action or way of doing things that has become established by a person or a group as the result of being repeated over a period of time.*[47]

What do we mean by its arts?
> *Any form of human activity that is the product of and appeals primary to the imagination...drawing, painting, sculpture, architecture, poetry, music and dancing.*[48]

What are its conveniences?
> *All the effects, ways, and tools of a people used to accomplish work and activity in an expedient fashion.*[49]

Also, we need to define the terms, *Cultural Forms* and *Meanings*.

Cultural Forms;
> *Any ceremony, ritual, particular way of doing things, which teach and guide the people in a culturally acceptable way of life. The form itself is the physical action that serves as a vehicle to carry the meaning.*[50]

---

[47] ibid. Page 31
[48] ibid. Page 31
[49] ibid. Page 32
[50] ibid. Page 33

Meanings are;
*The unwritten rules that establish proper behavior for people within their particular culture.*[51]

How do we process cultural forms and meaning in light of the gospel and the Scriptures?

A historically accepted missiological principle taught in higher educational institutions is that the issue of *Cultural Forms and Meanings* should be approached and evaluated in one of three distinctly different ways.

1. *Some cultural forms can be kept and a new meaning applied to it.*
2. *Other cultural forms need to be changed, and a new meaning applied to it.*
3. *Still other cultural forms are not acceptable at all, because those forms stand in direct conflict to biblical principles.*[52]

Where the third kind of forms are found, they need to be *abandoned completely* by the believers in that culture.

*These principles are now commonly being challenged in higher educational institutions impacted by the*

---

[51] ibid. Page 33

[52] ibid. Page 33

> *Redeeming of Culture movement that teaches all cultural forms are neutral, and thus can be transformed and used in Christian worship.*[53]

When we come to Christ, *Indigenous Faith* begins a lifelong journey into processing how to do life. The filter we used to use in our pre-Christian lives is no longer applicable to the believer. That must now be dismantled and put under the authority of Christ and revealed Scripture. The biblical grid must now replace the old. It will instruct the believer consistently in every tribe, language, people, and nation.

When properly applied, every culture is left with no choice but to abandon the sacred objects of traditional theologies. In that way, Red, Yellow, Black, and White believers in Christ must respond alike in this crucial act of obedience. This is a *key consistency* to be found in the *Kingdom of God*. What is joyfully different, God honoring, and provides *Kingdom diversity,* is when believers preserve the parts of their cultures that do not conflict with biblical guidelines. They keep the forms while giving them new meaning which glorifies God.

As an example, our North American tribes bestow great honor on our elders. They are celebrated as they continue to influence the community. They usually get first dibs at community feasts. This cultural form and meaning clearly enjoys biblical endorsement. The new meaning given not

---

[53] ibid. Page 34

only honors the elder but finds a way to honor the work of God in their life as well.

In other parts of the culture we discover forms that need to be changed because they violate biblical teaching.

We also uncover cultural forms and meanings that are offensive to God, such as Old Testament child sacrifices, etc. Whenever found, they are to be abandoned because the practice clearly violates Scripture and is totally offensive to a Holy God.

This is the true Body of Christ at work that Jesus died to redeem, empower, and use. *Critical contextualization* is being applied while *syncretism* is rejected.

Key to this new pattern of living is to become a committed student of God's Word, cultivating a hunger for truth, and discovering it in the pages of the Bible. As we read and apply His Word, we lay building blocks one on top of each other for a healthy biblical life.

Look back at the Scriptures uncovered in this book alone. Applying the truths of these few verses will help jump start your life in Christ as you process how to live God honoring *Indigenous Faith*.

It also impacts our corporate relationship with Him as well.

Jesus said these words to the woman at the well, in John 4:23-24;

*Yet a time is coming and has now come when the true worshipers will worship the Father in the Spirit and in truth, for they are the kind of worshipers the Father seeks. God is spirit, and his worshipers must worship in the Spirit and in truth.*

How do I apply this passage to my corporate relationship with God and His people?

If I am to worship God in a way that pleases Him, I must do so in the Spirit and in truth. *In the Spirit* helps us understand the energy of true worship. The "S" is capitalized. When that happens, Scripture is referring to the Holy Spirit and not the human or any other kind of spirit.

The Holy Spirit is crucial to the life of the believer. He also is a *come down* part of the Trinity, arriving on the Day of Pentecost over 2,000 years ago and remains in the world to this day. His role is to fill every believer in Christ with power from on high.

Christ gives His followers something no human religion does - His indwelling Presence that brings the holiness and power of God into a human life.

Colossians 1:27 puts it this way;

*To them God has chosen to make known among the Gentiles the glorious riches of this mystery, which is Christ in you, the hope of glory.*

Imperative to the believer is to be filled with the Holy Spirit on a day by day basis. There is no way to live out *Indigenous Faith* without Him.

Ephesians 5:17-19;

*Therefore do not be foolish, but understand what the Lord's will is. Do not get drunk on wine, which leads to debauchery. Instead, be filled with the Spirit, speaking to one another with psalms, hymns, and songs from the Spirit.*

There is a posture of humility we must have as we worship God. We surrender ourselves over to the Holy Spirit to controls our thoughts, words, and deeds. True worship sets aside any distractions, worries, and cares, as we give ourselves totally over in adoration to the King of kings and Lord of lords.

But there is also the word *truth* in this verse. If I am going to be a true worshipper of Jesus, my worship has to be based on truth. Where do we find truth? It is waiting to be discovered in only one place, in the pages of God's Holy Word.

*Your Word is truth (John 17:17).*

This passage tells us only two things are necessary to worship God in the way that pleases Him; the power of the Holy Spirit and the truth of God's Word. Do I need an organ, piano, or guitar to worship God? The answer is absolutely not! These neutral instruments are only *accessories* and not necessary for true worship to take place.

## The Importance of Open Communication

I would encourage leaders of local churches, denominations, mission organizations, etc., to meet together with local indigenous believers to evaluate their unique culture and traditions in light of biblical doctrine.

In doing so, commit to applying the truths of Scripture as top priority. Establish an honest and clear evaluation of what that culture's sacred objects are and biblically evaluate its cultural forms and meanings. Seek to determine which of those forms can be kept, changed, or needing to be abandoned. I trust the truths in this book will be of help to indigenous believers worldwide as you seek to do this. We also have developed some other tools to aid in that process.

Not long ago I was privileged to teach *Indigenous Faith* at a Christian college. In attendance were indigenous believers, pastors, missionaries, and others interested in the subject. We recorded the six sessions live in both audio and high definition video formats.

Those Audio CD and DVD sets are now available for order on our website, tribalrescue.com. We also have student workbooks and a leader's guide to help take your congregation or small group into an in-depth study on

*Indigenous Faith.* Each of the six sessions end with *Points to Ponder* questions that help direct discussion on the materials presented in that session. We would encourage you to order a set today.

Sacred objects, customs, arts, and conveniences differ from tribe to tribe. That is why I do not offer a blanket statement that would be applicable to all tribes worldwide. Instead, this book is written to help any culture evaluate its own unique traditions and spiritual ways by processing them through a consistently applied biblical filter.

There needs to be evaluations done at the local level among believers in every indigenous people group. The larger Body of Christ can be of great help in the process and should never see themselves as automatically relegated to the seat of a spectator. The same Bible guides and governs both. Healthy intercultural interchanges can be of great service to this interdependent Body of Christ.

C&MA U.S. Native ministry has been the better for our intentional journey into evaluating the indigenous cultures we work with through our Task Force's effort. It still stands today as the filter by which we process the cultures we minister in.

So then, what were the lessons we learned in our journey to define *Indigenous Faith?*

First, we determined to do this work together, as a team, with both Native and non-Native involvement. Our task force was diverse, both racially, tribally, educationally, and generationally.

A former Navajo medicine man, Pete Greyeyes, stood shoulder to shoulder with Dr. Keith M. Bailey, a well-respected theologian and denominational leader. Each man of God brought incredible cultural and theological insight to the table in their own unique ways.

Native leaders like Herman Williams (*Navajo*) and Mike Owen (*Dakotah*) and myself (*Ojibwe*), interacted with one of our long time and respected cross-cultural workers, Rev. Doug Haskins, in the discussions as well. We all had perspective and opinions to offer, and were all treated with equal respect and honor. It drew us together in a remarkable way during this important gathering.

We prayed and even wept together because of the seriousness of the issues we were facing. Ultimately, we came to agree that the *Redeeming of Culture* doctrine could not be viewed as sound doctrine and must be avoided by our indigenous churches and believers. We did not arrive at that determination lightly but with gravity and much heaviness of heart.

The seriousness of the issue came through clearly when our report was later presented to the workers and lay delegates from our Native Alliance congregations. After clarifying the task force's positions and answering any remaining questions the report and recommendations were put to a vote.

One hundred percent were in favor of the findings and recommendations that continue to guide the Native Alliance Association of churches to this day.

Both cultural and theological understanding is needed to do this kind of work. We found that the best cultural insights came from the perspectives of our well-respected Navajo elders, Herman Williams and Pete Greyeyes. It is important to bring to the table, if at all possible, first generation Christians like them, who were raised in their culture and traditions, yet whose identity and significance are in alignment with that of the Apostle Paul.

These godly men were fully aware of the cultural forms and meanings at play. They could identify specifically what were the sacred objects of their tribe, and what cultural forms could be kept, changed, or needed to be abandoned.

On the theological side, applying the same filter is imperative in looking for biblically solid veterans of the faith who rightfully divide the Word of truth and maintain a high view of Scripture.

Do not make the mistake of going down the trail of finding theologians who embrace the contemporary shift to an existential or more culturally based hermeneutic that has become the new fad. They will only affirm to you that Scripture is not the basis on which to make such determinations, while encouraging you to allow culture to define, interpret, and apply the Scriptures.

In our Task Force's discussions, both theological and cultural considerations emerged that became the template by which we evaluated the teaching of the *Redeeming the Culture* movement. Below are key summary statements that we came to affirm back then and which we continue to stand on today. It is these truths that God honoring *Indigenous Faith* must be built upon.

Because of the foundational truth of *Christology,* there is no other way to the Father but through Christ. Indigenous believers must abandon the using of any sacred object or mediator between man and the spirit realm.

1 Timothy 2:5 makes it clear that;

> ...there is one God and one mediator between God and mankind, the man Christ Jesus.

Because of this, smudging is not for the believer in Christ. Smoke of any nature is no longer the mediator between mankind and the spirit world. Only Christ holds that position of honor.

We must not go down the road of Nadab and Abihu of old by offering unauthorized fire before God in personal or corporate worship.

A.W. Tozer noted;

*As Christian believers, we must stand together against some things. So, if you hear anyone saying that A.W. Tozer preaches a good deal that is negative, just smile and agree: "That is because he preaches the Bible!" Here are some of the things we oppose: we are against the many modern idols that have been allowed to creep into the churches; we are against the "unauthorized fire" that is being offered on the altars of the Lord; we are against the modern gods that are being adopted into our sanctuaries...God asks us to stand boldly against anything or anyone who hurts or hinders this New Testament body of Christians. Where the church is not healed it will wither. The Word of God is the antibiotic that alone can destroy the virus that would plague the life of the church!*[54]

His insightful words led my wife, LaDonna, whom I have served with together in over forty years of ministry, to post recently;

*We are looking more and more like the compromising Church. The Church is stepping outside God's boundary of protection and dabbling in things that will drive God far from us, because He will not share His affections with the world religions and their ways. God help us to stay true to the inerrant Word of God. He is coming soon like He said He would! The world will be happy to be rid of us, along*

---

[54] Excerpts taken from A.W. Tozer's sermon, *The Worldly "Virus".*

*with the presence of the Holy Spirit. Chaos upon chaos will be the norm then. Hang in there Church! Be ready!*

We also agreed with Paul on the importance of the new identity and significance afforded the believer. Biblical identity must take precedence over our previous cultural identity and significance.

Our high view of Scripture affirms valid biblical interpretation can only be arrived at by utilizing a grammatico-historical hermeneutic. Proper interpretation rests on the consideration of the literary context of the passage, the historical background, geographical features, and grammar of the text.

The doctrine of *Separation,* as outlined by Paul in 2 Corinthians 6:14-18, prohibits the believer in Christ from redeeming objects from our old spirit worship and practices.

We affirmed that in the *Kingdom of God*, there will be similarities in worship and living among all believers worldwide because of a shared commitment to biblical principles and doctrine. Culture is no longer our pursuit. Christ is.

The sacred objects of the nations are never neutral and unaffected by the powers of darkness in the demonic world. Animistic people understand clearly the existence and power of the spirit world and know there is resident power connected with the sacred objects we historically have revered and appeased.

For the believer, we must abandon any usage of sacred objects in our personal lives, our homes, and in our houses of worship. Understanding this reality will keep us from being affected by the powers of darkness in our personal life and will keep the house of God clean from any syncretistic practices that *drive God far from His sanctuary.*

We further affirmed that worship that is not focused on Jesus is not true worship of the Creator. Most if not all indigenous people are creationists. When the creators found in indigenous religions worldwide are worship it is not the same as biblical worship of the One true Creator of the universe as revealed in the Word of God.

We also concluded that there is not enough revelation of God in *General Revelation* to bring salvation to any nation. Knowledge of general revelation does not solve the spiritual need of any nation but only leaves them *without excuse (Romans 1:20).*

That is why *Special Revelation* was needed to bring the hope of the gospel. Genuine knowledge or heart for God, as expressed in religion apart from Christ and the gospel, is not enough to save a person.

We also looked at the history of The C&MA (US) which has included missionary work among indigenous people around the globe since its inception in the late 1800's.

Dr. Peter Nanfelt, president of The Christian and Missionary Alliance at the time our task force met, weighed in with some helpful guidance in rightfully dividing the Word of truth on these matters. He stated;

> *I think we can probably adopt many things from non-Christian cultures that are acceptable. The hymnology of Irian Jaya, for example, consists of chants. The Dyaks in Kalimantan use coconut milk for communion because they have no grapes. The examples are endless. But we need the wisdom of God to know when animistic beliefs have so invaded the culture that those aspects of culture need to be abandoned.*[55]

He further cautioned;

> *Unfortunately, there will probably always be debates about what cultural activities have animistic meanings and overtures and which are strictly neutral. If we have any serious questions we should probably take the more cautious position.*[56]

That was very good advice for us then and still helps us as we sort out the supernatural in our cultures today.

In the days before our Task Force addressed these issues, some syncretistic forms of worship were being introduced in one of our Native Alliance congregations by

---

[55] ibid. Page 30

[56] ibid. Page 30

a non-Native pastor sympathetic to such practices. It was met with Alliance leadership confronting the issue without apology. In doing so, they stopped the advancement of it, even though the worker garnered local television and other media coverage as they protested outside one of our suburban Alliance churches for an extended period of time.

C&MA leaders had no choice but to apply church discipline and the worker eventually was removed and his credentials revoked.

As awkward and painful as that process was, it was the right thing to do in handling this form of false teaching. I commend The Alliance leadership for their courage and commitment to the authority of Scripture, even while facing huge backlash from a not-so-friendly media. May today's defenders of biblical truth be encouraged in the battles we face as we remember those who have gone on before us. They modeled an unwavering commitment to God's Word and so must we.

## Some Helpful Examples

Several good examples of proper critical contextualization emerged as we applied the process outlined above. They came from the Navajo Nation and are examples of how to rightfully apply God's Word to cultural forms and meanings.

These examples serve to illustrate how you, your fellow believers, and church leadership can process your indigenous culture in the light of God's Word.

### *Option 1: Keep the Form, Change the Meaning.*
### *Navajo Baby Laugh[57]:*

Among many tribes, the believers have retained various cultural forms that do not conflict with the Bible. One example is the Navajo *Baby Laugh.* An important time in the development of an infant is when it is finally able to laugh for the first time. The importance of this milestone to the Navajo is their belief that a child is not complete until it laughs.

Traditionally, a celebration is held to commerate this major event. One of the more interesting aspects is that the person who makes the baby laugh is the one who has to foot the bill for the celebration, which can turn into a very costly experience. In other words, while the baby is the one laughing, the host is the one crying! The *Baby Laugh* celebration unites the community and continues to reaffirm the uniqueness of the Navajo people.

In the church setting, Navajo believers also have baby laugh celebrations. Navajo pastors use such an occasion to present biblical principles, while the elder believers

---
[57] ibid. Page 35.

admonish parents to raise the child in the Lord. It is a joyous time of celebration for the church, including feasting, and rejoicing in the Lord for the gift of life. Sometimes, this is when the parents offer the child back to the Lord in a baby dedication.

This celebration does not stand in conflict with any biblical teaching. It is a good illustration of keeping a cultural form while giving it new meaning consistent with biblical truth.

*Option 2: Change the Form, Change the Meaning*
*Navajo Puberty Ceremony:*

An example of critical contextualization being done in a strongly traditional culture would be the puberty ceremony of the Navajos.

In the traditional (non-Christian) puberty ceremony, which lasts for four nights, oversight is provided by the elder matriarch of the family. There is teaching of the role of the woman in the family and extended clan system, and a strong emphasis is placed on the role of the woman in the family as the giver of life. The blessing of womanhood means that life will be perpetuated to the next generation. Corn is used in the ceremonies, and it represents reproduction. The girl going through puberty becomes a mediator of *Changing Woman*, who is a central spirit of the Navajo belief system.

During one of the days the girl places her hands on the shoulders of the people gathered, and by doing so, passes a spiritual blessing to them from *Changing Woman*. Each morning, before the sun comes up, the girl runs ever-increasing distances, which symbolizes a strong work ethic.

Many Navajo believers see great value in a puberty celebration which includes training, teaching, and instructing young people in developing godly character. Navajo believers concluded (take out - who embrace using the puberty ceremony) that in order to utilize this cultural practice, it was not enough to just supply a new meaning to the old form used in the traditional way. They had to change not only the meaning, but change the form itself.

The Christian puberty celebration is a one-night event, where there is biblical teaching on godly character development in the life of a woman. An older Christian woman assumes the role of overseer of the instruction to the girl which is in accordance with biblical principles.

> *Titus 2:3-5 Likewise, teach the older women to be reverent in the way they live, not to be slanderers or addicted to much wine, but to teach what is good. Then they can train the younger women to love their husbands and children, to be self-controlled and pure, to be busy at home, to be kind, and to be subject to their husbands, so that no one will malign the word of God.*

The morning after the teaching, there is a feast for all in attendance. In this way, the church is viewed in the role of the extended family of the young woman. The young woman often will give gifts at this time to those who participated in sharing instruction and wisdom. Sometimes the girl will run, symbolic of a good work ethic.

For any person observing the two ceremonies, the distinct differences would be clearly evident. There is no way the two ceremonies could be confused. Not only has the meaning been changed, but the form had to change as well.

The intent of the traditional ceremony is to maintain harmony and balance with the spirit world, and to announce to the community that the young woman was now available for marriage.

The intent of the Christian ceremony is to instruct the woman in godly character development and celebrate the role of the individual in the life of the church.

*Chapter Ten*

# ADDRESSING THE IMPLICATIONS

### A Biblical Response to Richard Twiss' Statement

IT HAS BEEN QUITE A JOURNEY INTO GOD'S WORD AS WE have sought to *contend for the faith that was once for all entrusted to God's holy people.* That is, my friend, the only standard that enables us to live out God honoring and biblically aligned *Indigenous Faith.*

In chapter 2, we set the table by introducing a quote from Richard Twiss that addressed the personal side of *Indigenous Faith.* Remember what he stated?

> *I was made to burn and destroy all my tribal carvings, eagle feathers, and my dance outfit because the pastor told me now that I was a Christian, old things passed away and all things became new, which meant all my Native cultural ways needed to be replaced with Euro-American cultural ways. Then I was told I could no longer participate in our Native gatherings, dances or*

ceremonies because they were of the devil and full of idolatry. They even told me my Native drum was an idol and full of spirits, so I burned it and learned the guitar instead. Now I am no longer a Native in my culture. I am an anglicized Christian in American culture. The Bible has been used to colonize my soul.

Indicting words, indeed!

How, then, are we to look at these words and evaluate them? The only way a believer in Christ can do this is through the prism of God's Holy Word! There is no other option, especially if we maintain a high view of Scripture and see God's Word as *the divine and only rule of Christian faith and practice.*

I would like to break down his quote into three parts and offer my response to each by applying the principles laid out in *Indigenous Faith*. I pray it would serve as a template for you to evaluate your own culture, traditions, and religious upbringings that once guided you before coming to faith in Christ.

Let us look at the first part of Richard's quote. He stated;

*I was made to burn and destroy all my tribal carvings, eagle feathers, and my dance outfit because the pastor told me now that I was a Christian, old things passed away and all things became new, which meant all my*

> *Native cultural ways needed to be replaced with Euro-American cultural ways...*

Using the searchlight of Scripture any *ethnos* will have to admit some, if not much of their cultural ways, do not line up with biblical truth. It is those things we need to destroy and distance ourselves from, especially as it relates to our sacred objects.

I cannot take you anywhere in Scripture to show you where God's people redeemed the sacred objects of the other nations around them, and the blessing of God ensued. It surely did not happen when they made their own idols, such as the golden calf, as described in Exodus 32.

> *When the people saw that Moses was so long in coming down from the mountain, they gathered around Aaron and said, "Come, make us gods who will go before us. As for this fellow Moses who brought us up out of Egypt, we do not know what has happened to him." Aaron answered them, "Take off the gold earrings that your wives, your sons and your daughters are wearing, and bring them to me." So all the people took off their earrings and brought them to Aaron. He took what they handed him and made it into an idol cast in the shape of a calf, fashioning it with a tool. Then they said, "These are your gods, Israel, who brought you up out of Egypt." When Aaron saw this, he built an altar in front of the calf and announced,*

"Tomorrow there will be a festival to the Lord." So the next day the people rose early and sacrificed burnt offerings and presented fellowship offerings. Afterward they sat down to eat and drink and got up to indulge in revelry. Then the Lord said to Moses, "Go down, because your people, whom you brought up out of Egypt, have become corrupt. They have been quick to turn away from what I commanded them and have made themselves an idol cast in the shape of a calf. They have bowed down to it and sacrificed to it and have said, 'These are your gods, Israel, who brought you up out of Egypt.' "I have seen these people," the Lord said to Moses, "and they are a stiff-necked people. Now leave me alone so that my anger may burn against them and that I may destroy them. Then I will make you into a great nation."

We have seen many Scriptural passages that show the blessing of God on His people when they destroyed the idols, sacred objects, and detestable images of their own.

Syncretists are left to answer the burning question, *When and where did God's attitude and actions change regarding sacred objects in the New or Older Testament where He now sanctions and blesses them in the life of the believer?* Where is the Scriptural proof for that kind of monumental change in heaven's *come down* theology?

Syncretists may want to make the case that it is only in the Old Testament where these admonitions were made.

We are now living in the New Testament age, they might argue, which is totally different from the Old.

While it can be debated there are differences between the Old Testament law and New Testament grace, I do not believe the heart of God has changed one bit on his anger with syncretistic behaviors of His people. Paul distinctly weaves the Old and New Testaments together in Acts 28:23-30, where he states;

> *They arranged to meet Paul on a certain day, and came in even larger numbers to the place where he was staying. He witnessed to them from morning till evening, explaining about the kingdom of God, and from the Law of Moses and from the Prophets he tried to persuade them about Jesus. Some were convinced by what he said, but others would not believe. They disagreed among themselves and began to leave after Paul had made this final statement: "The Holy Spirit spoke the truth to your ancestors when he said through Isaiah the prophet: 'Go to this people and say, "You will be ever hearing but never understanding; you will be ever seeing but never perceiving." For this people's heart has become calloused, they hardly hear with their ears, and they have closed their eyes. Otherwise they might see with their eyes, hear with their ears, understand with their hearts and turn, and I would heal them.' "Therefore I want you to know that God's salvation has been sent to the Gentiles, and they will listen!" For two*

*whole years Paul stayed there in his own rented house and welcomed all who came to see him.*

In light of this, I ask those who embrace a *Redeeming of Culture* theology to take me to chapter and verse that shows biblical blessing on the redeeming of sacred objects! Of course, if you argue from the perspective of a culture hermeneutic you can arrive at that position quite easily. The only problem with that position is your authority is culture and not the Word of God. I can't do that, and I pray neither will you, my friend.

Mr. Twiss is wrong in the perception of replacing Native cultural ways with Euro-American cultural ways. As we've seen in this book, we are to subject our Native cultural ways to the new higher culture of the *Kingdom of God*. In this way, there will be both *key similarities* and *key diversities* with other believers in Christ in nations and cultures who are living in biblical obedience.

Based on the principles of Christ's *Kingdom culture*, my new identity and significance must now take precedence over my old one. The old was anchored in my pre-Christian cultural upbringing and traditional ways. While human cultures and ways still can contribute to our lives as Christians, those ways must now be aligned in accordance with biblical truth and always subordinate to the principles of the *Kingdom of God*. This reality is true for every person who follows Christ regardless of their human culture and past identity.

As believers in Christ we have found something far greater than a cultural identity. We have found *the surpassing worth of knowing Christ Jesus my Lord, for whose sake I have lost all things* (Philippians 3:4-11).

An Anglo-American who comes to Christ today must also abandon the sin-stained culture and traditions that are resident within his modern Western culture and upbringing.

He also is called to this higher level of living. This mutually shared *Kingdom culture*, based solely on the revealed Scriptures, is the new way of living for every soul surrendered to Christ. His abandoned idols may look different from that of an animistic person, but all must be abandoned in exchange for allegiance and commitment to Christ and Christ alone.

As an example, when a Wall Street executive or high-powered attorney from mainstream America repents of sin and now desires to walk in biblical obedience, he now is called to live like his Ojibwe counterpart who also has found salvation through Jesus Christ. We are mutually guided, as adopted kids in the *Kingdom of God*, by a shared value system as taught by God's Holy Word. It is not a horizontal cultural shift to another sin-stained culture that Christ calls us to. It is only when we are raised up vertically, into His Kingdom, that we can enjoy the fullness and great blessing our life in Christ affords.

An important difference between Native Americans and America's European immigrants is we have had the gospel for a relatively shorter period of time - just over five-hundred years. Whereas, the gospel has influenced European cultures for over two millennia.

Time has its way of reshaping a culture, people, or group, whether that be for good or for evil. The longer a culture is exposed to the truth of the Scriptures and applies its principles, it will find itself moving further and further away from the practices that the Creator of heaven and earth detests.

Remember the lessons from Israel's own journey over the centuries. When they lived in obedience to God and His *special revelation* to them, it resulted in the blessing and favor of God. When they chose to be disobedient, the judgement of God followed, even though they maintained their special relationship with God as His chosen people.

God does not see Christians from Western civilization in a more preferential way than He does of indigenous believers who come to faith out of first, second, or third world countries. Indigenous believers have as much to offer the *Kingdom of God* as the educated, wealthy, or even powerfully influential brothers and sisters in Christ who have been used of God for centuries. As I stated in *Whiteman's Gospel, God's greatest work has never been done by the strong and mighty, but through the underdogs*!

1 Corinthians 1:26-29 reminds us that all have an equal seat at the table of God. If some folk think they are

something special because of an earthly status, they may want to reconsider that posture as Paul reminds us;

*Brothers and sisters, think of what you were when you were called. Not many of you were wise by human standards; not many were influential; not many were of noble birth. But God chose the foolish things of the world to shame the wise; God chose the weak things of the world to shame the strong. God chose the lowly things of this world and the despised things—and the things that are not—to nullify the things that are, so that no one may boast before him.*

Biblically speaking, there are only three groups of people living simultaneously across the globe at any time in human history. This reality has been in existence since the plains of Shinar.

It is found in Joshua 24:15;

*But if serving the Lord seems undesirable to you, then choose for yourselves this day whom you will serve, whether the gods your ancestors served beyond the Euphrates, or the gods of the Amorites, in whose land you are living. But as for me and my household, we will serve the Lord.*

The three options for living are clear. You can choose to serve the *gods of your ancestors*, choose to serve the *gods of the people in the land you are now living in,* or choose to serve the Lord.

*But as for me and my household, we will serve the Lord!*

The next part of Richard's quote says;

*...then I was told I could no longer participate in our Native gatherings, dances or ceremonies because they were of the devil and full of idolatry. They even told me my Native drum was an idol and full of spirits, so I burned it and learned the guitar instead.*

Spiritism permeates Native traditional culture. This requires Native Christians to evaluate our gatherings, dances, and ceremonies in light of the higher *Kingdom of God.*

The *Doctrine of Separation* must be the filter we use to answer the question of our continued involvement in such gatherings, ceremonies, etc.

2 Cor. 6:14-16 reminds us;

*Do not be yoked together with unbelievers. For what do righteousness and wickedness have in common? Or what fellowship can light have with darkness? What harmony is there between Christ and Belial? What does a believer have in common with an unbeliever? What agreement is there between the temple of God and idols? For we are the temple of the living God. As God has said: "I will live with them and walk among them, and I will be their God, and they will be my people."*

It cannot be denied that our tribal gatherings are not just *social events but profoundly spiritual* in nature and routinely involve the utilization of sacred objects. As Christians we must address critical and important realities in determining whether or not to attend or participate.

Here is the filter I use to process my own upbringing in light of my new life in Christ.

First, I ask myself, *Would it please God if I participate in an event or ceremony where sacred objects are being used?*

At this point one might be tempted to rationalize that since we do not personally worship those sacred objects or surmise that they do not have any effect on us, why not attend or participate?

Again, God's Word trumps those rationalizations as we place ourselves under Scripture's authority over our lives.

I have concluded that my active participation in such events would not bear the blessing and sanction of God based on His Word's clear instruction to me. As Martin Luther said, *My conscience is captive to the Word of God!*

This can be a painful process for those whom culture and tradition are of utmost importance. We are often pressed to conform and left with the potential of ridicule and scorn from even close friends and family. These are often not easy decisions to make. In the valley of decision, we must go back to what the Apostle Paul stated about his identity and significance in Christ. When we do so, courage and boldness from God's Holy Spirit encourages and strengthens us. We will continually have to assess what the priorities of our lives are as we face the same challenge the next time the ceremony or event is held.

Secondly, to drill down even deeper, the question needs to be asked, *Do I have the freedom in Christ, based on the Doctrine of Separation, to even attend, even if I do not participate?*

This is a bit more of a challenging *gray area* to answer. I do acknowledge there are believers in Christ who are dear friends of mine that hold to the position that they can.

Often their rationalization is culturally based more than biblically based. What is needed at this point is to apply the contextualization options outlined earlier in the book.

The question is, in keeping in alignment with God's Word, *Do I keep the form and change the meaning, must I change the form and give it a new meaning, or must I abandon the form entirely because there is not any biblical support for my attending?*

The same filter of God's Word needs to shape our decisions, even if it does put us in a culturally awkward position by doing so. Our people do view the drum as sacred along with other paraphernalia used in these events. We know God's clear position on those objects.

The question needing an answer might be as simple as, *Is getting a good piece of fry bread enough to please the Lord by my attending an event where sacred objects are front and center?*

Remember, this is where the spirits are being called upon. This is much more than an issue of personal conscience for each of us as indigenous followers of Christ. It must be seen as an act of obedience to God flowing from a heart of love for Him and His Word.

Some might say that there are conflicting biblical passages that argue both sides of this coin. The Corinthian passage articulating the *Doctrine of Separation* argues against attending, while other biblical accounts, such as Jesus eating with the tax collectors, seem to authorize and bless our attendance at such events.

Mark 2:15-17 states;

*While Jesus was having dinner at Levi's house, many tax collectors and sinners were eating with him and his disciples, for there were many who followed him. When the teachers of the law who were Pharisees saw him eating with the sinners and tax collectors, they asked his disciples: "Why does he eat with tax collectors and sinners?" On hearing this, Jesus said to them, "It is not the healthy who need a doctor, but the sick. I have not come to call the righteous, but sinners."*

I acknowledge that these passages speak to the issue from what could be construed as differing points of view. Allow me to offer one thought on the Lord eating with the tax collectors (whom we all agree are definitely sinners) that is relevant to our discussion.

Does anybody find reference to the utilization of sacred objects in the serving of the meal or in the events of the gathering? I sure don't. In light of God's *top two of His top ten list*, the issue of believers intentionally attending events that involve sacred objects is of great importance as we process the gray areas of life.

*Indigenous Faith* understands the challenge of being *in the world* while not being *a part of the world*, especially when that world is animistic in nature.

John 15:19 puts it this way;

*If you belonged to the world, it would love you as its own. As it is, you do not belong to the world, but I have chosen you out of the world. That is why the world hates you.*

In John 17:14-16, Christ's High Priestly prayer to the Father for us further states;

> *I have given them your word and the world has hated them, for they are not of the world any more than I am of the world. My prayer is not that you take them out of the world but that you protect them from the evil one. They are not of the world, even as I am not of it. Sanctify them by the truth; your word is truth. As you sent me into the world, I have sent them into the world. For them I sanctify myself, that they too may be truly sanctified.*

How else will lost people know about Christ unless we are actively engaged in our communities? Our home folk need to see Christ's love in and through us as we present to them the hope and salvation He offers. That is crucially important! We must strike a healthy balance, however, between being productive community members who reflect Christ well, while avoiding compromising our faith by engaging in activities that do not line up with biblical truth.

Thirdly, an important outcome to consider that has clear biblical comment is, *What do I do if my actions cause other believers to stumble or fall in their Christian walk?*

1 Corinthians 8:9 instructs us;

> *Be careful, however, that the exercise of your rights does not become a stumbling block to the weak.*

True godliness and humility will always seek the good of others and is often achieved at our own expense.

Now back to Mr. Twiss' statement where he blames non-Native pastors for referring to his *drum as an idol and full of spirits*.

Any serious evaluation of Native culture would have to affirm that our Native drums are spiritually empowered sacred objects. The source of those beliefs, though, do not originate from the intolerable and insensitive quotes of Anglo missionaries and pastors, but from the myriad of traditional Native leaders who clearly articulate such claims, as noted earlier in this book.

The blame game will never get us far in the advancement of holiness in our lives. If blaming the Anglos truly was his conviction, he had to bypass the real definers of this Native theological centerpiece. This once again leads us to the necessity of applying biblical truth to this issue as well.

If our culture honors and reveres objects as sacred and empowered by spirits, how can I conclude that I can redeem them for God honoring worship? I will never reach that conclusion based on the revealed Word of God. This matter must never be trivialized by contemporary believers in Christ. A clear line in the sand must be drawn for a follower of Christ in this important issue.

Richard concludes by stating;

> ...now I am no longer a Native in my culture. I am an anglicized Christian in American culture. The Bible has been used to colonize my soul.

My conscience is clear and my heart is at peace by holding to the positions I maintain on these issues. I am still a Native person because in God's Sovereignty that is who He created me to be. It was from the White Earth Band of Ojibwe, of which I am an enrolled member, that He chose to redeem me and make me His own. I am still an enrolled member of my earthly tribe, with all the privileges it affords and challenges it brings. But I am also a member of a heavenly tribe, whose chief is the mighty *Chief Cornerstone*! The Apostle Paul puts it this way in Ephesians 2:20;

> ...built on the foundation of the apostles and prophets, with Christ Jesus himself as the chief cornerstone.

I am one of those spoken of in Revelation 5:9. This incredible verse speaks of Christ, His death, burial, and resurrection, and all that He has accomplished for me in the following words;

> *You are worthy to take the scroll and to open its seals, because you were slain, and with your blood you*

*purchased for God persons from every tribe and language and people and nation.*

I am eternally indebted to God for His grace that enabled me to become one of His own, redeemed *from every tribe, language, people, and nation.* Everything changed for me on August 3, 1971 when I surrendered my life to Christ and He became my Savior. As I now live for Him, I no longer am conformed to this world's ways.

Paul says to the Roman believers in Romans 12:2;

*Do not conform to the pattern of this world, but be transformed by the renewing of your mind. Then you will be able to test and approve what God's will is—his good, pleasing and perfect will.*

There are many things that I still enjoy, embrace, and celebrate from my Ojibwe heritage that are not contrary to the truths of the revealed Word of God. I continue to honor our elders because that is not only a cultural value, but a biblical one as well. Fry bread *will not* be forsaken by this Ojibwe believer, although its grease may add years to my eternal life! Every time I eat Green Chile Pork Stew I am so thankful that I was created a Gentile! On and on the examples could go, but I think you get the point!

Finally, I cannot accept Twiss' notion that I am now an anglicized Christian in American culture. I am a Spirit-filled

Christian living in alignment with the principles of the highest level of living available to man. I now live and exist in this amazing *Kingdom of God* and its way of life as outlined in God's Holy Word.

The Bible has not been used to *colonized my soul*. The Bible has been used to *liberate my soul*, enabling me to live a holy life that is well pleasing in His sight, as I follow His clear teachings and instructions! For the believer in Jesus Christ there is no better way to live than keeping our wigwam camped close to the Word of God!

### Practical Theological and Cultural Guidelines

Our Native Alliance Task Force did a very helpful thing at the conclusion of our report. We posited a summary of very practical *Theological and Cultural Guidelines* designed to help indigenous believers in the process of critical contextualization.

*Indigenous Faith* has gone much deeper in developing the theological framework by which we process culture. Both works lead to the very same conclusions and guidelines by which to live by.

These guidelines will help put feet to the theological and cultural framework presented in *Indigenous Faith*.

## Theological Guidelines

- Because of the foundational truth that outside of Jesus Christ, there is no other way to the Father/Creator, but by Him, the native believer in Jesus Christ must abandon the usage of any traditional (or contemporary) object that would serve as mediator between man and the spirit realm.
- True worship of Christ must be both spiritual and it must be based on truth. The Holy Spirit is the energy of worship, and the truth of God's Word is the substance of true worship. This means that no objects are necessary for true worship to take place. Objects we may elect to use in worship must conform to Christ's principles of worship.
- The foundation of our identity as believers must be a biblical identity, rather than a secular or cultural concept of identity. For the Christian, biblical identity takes precedence over any other definition of identity.
- Since we believe that the Bible is the inerrant, infallible, inspired Word of God valid interpretation must rest on the grammatico-historical approach to hermeneutics. Proper interpretation of Scripture calls for the consideration of the literary context of the passage, the historical background, geographical features, and the grammar of the text.

- The idea of redeeming objects from spirit worship for Christian worship cannot be reconciled with the biblical position on separation from such objects and practices.
- Christian worship is distinctly new and from God, and is not dependent on anyone's culture. Though there are different styles of worship among different people, all worship must conform to the biblical conditions and parameters for worship. They are the same for all people who come to Christ.
- Animism as a demonic system invades the culture of any people that embrace it. When there are converts from animism they do not need to renounce their culture. They need only to renounce the evil infestation of spirit worship, which God hates.
- The material artifacts (sacred objects) used by animists are never neutral, but dedicated to the demons. In most instances, they are actually indwelt by demons.
- Worship not focused on Jesus, is not true worship of the Creator. This is overlooking and denying the doctrine of the Trinity as active in the work of creation.
- The only hope open to any sinner anywhere at any time and any place is Christ, the Way, the Truth, and the Life. The Gospel of Christ is special revelation. Salvation is by God, Himself. His instruction is

to preach it to everybody in all the world, because Christ is the Savior of the world.
- Replacing or attempting to enhance Christ with any object, be it animate, inanimate, or even a living being is placing other gods before the One True God.

## *Cultural Guidelines*

- We have found no examples of Alliance churches and nationals embracing the "redeeming of sacred objects" used formerly in animistic practices and worship.
- Critical Contextualization is the process by which cultural forms and meanings are evaluated by the believers within the culture (not those from outside the culture), and determinations are made as to which cultural forms can be kept and a new meaning applied to it; which cultural forms need to be changed, and given new meaning; and which cultural forms are not acceptable at all, because those forms stand in direct conflict to biblical principles. By evaluating these cultural forms, different cultural forms are identified which can be used as a bridge to present the gospel message to a specific cultural group.
- When the church is truly abiding by the Scriptures, the church will be the instrument of God to positively

change, shape, and influence every human culture and system of thought it touches. Most importantly, it brings to a people God's only plan of salvation, resulting in restored harmony with God.
- The native church leadership must take the initiative in leading the native church through the process of receiving church worship and practice from outside our culture, as the starting point of developing true indigenous, biblically based worship. Each generation has the opportunity to contribute in this process, but sound biblical doctrine must be the defining principles that guide the church.
- In instances where we have serious questions or are unsure about whether or not cultural activities have animistic overtures, we should take the more cautious position.
- As long as western style hymnology does not conflict with biblical principles, and if the western style hymnology is meeting the needs of a particular native church, they should not feel obligated to move from western hymnology to a more indigenous hymnology. Western style hymnology, sung with their own unique native flavor, then, has become the indigenous form of worship for that church.
- The unique cultural expressions of any people group should never overshadow the importance of

each cultural group's relationship with the body of Christ at large.
- The syncretism we are opposed to is the integration of non-biblical native religious beliefs, practices and forms with biblical truth and faith in Christ.
- It is our strong belief that the key people best poised to lead the native church in the process of critical contextualization are the spiritually mature native Christian elders and leaders who have had personal experience in their respective cultures.
- A distinction needs to be made regarding the difference between cultural forms, and sacred objects. While cultural forms have the potential of remaining the same, being changed or being abandoned, sacred objects do not have this option. Biblically, they must be abandoned.
- We believe that the best equipped person to do critical contextualization of the traditional native culture would be a "First Generation Christian" who has come out of a traditional native culture. It is these men and women who are best able to see beyond the surface of the issues to the deeper implications of the role the spirit world and animism play in cultural forms and meanings.
- Assimilated, urbanized native people also can be first generation Christians, and as such, would be equipped for the process of applying biblical

principles to their own unique native culture. They will be evaluating a native culture that is in many ways different from its more traditional counterpart.
- Who contextualizes is as important as what is contextualized. You can only contextualize to the extent of your understanding of all the implications of a given culture.[58]

---

[58] ibid. Pages 52-26.

*Chapter Eleven*

# MY GAME CHANGER MOMENT

**I LEAVE YOU WITH ONE FINAL QUESTION.**

As you look throughout the Scriptures, where do you find all the nations together in one location in true worship of Jesus Christ? You cannot find it in the gospels. You do not find it in the book of Acts or anywhere in the Epistles written to the churches while they anxiously awaited Christ's glorious return to earth. The only place you can find it is in John's book of Revelation.

The setting is heaven. The specific place is the throne room of the King of kings, and Lord of lords. John looks and sees a multitude, far beyond what he can number.

He states in Revelation 7:9-11;

*After this I looked, and there before me was a great multitude that no one could count, from every nation, tribe, people and language, standing before the throne and before the Lamb. They were wearing white robes and were holding palm branches in their hands. And they cried out in a loud voice: "Salvation belongs to our God, who sits on the throne, and to the Lamb." All the angels were standing around the throne and around the elders and the four living creatures. They fell down on their faces before the throne and worshiped God, saying: "Amen! Praise and glory and wisdom and thanks and honor and power and strength be to our God for ever and ever. Amen!"*

John was able to identify the masses by their tribal and linguistic uniquenesses, *standing before the throne and before the Lamb.* Were they arrayed in their finest tribal garb at this monumental moment? It would only be right to show up to this gathering in our finest regalia, right? We always want to look our best by putting on our finest when something special is going on. So, where is the splendor and color of the various tribal regalia in full display that John saw in heaven?

The answer is it is nowhere to be found! In its place was a monochromatic uniformity of dress, that at first glance seems to be so unappealing and out of context for the tribes of the world!

But white robes? You gotta be kidding me! I am sure some of our indigenous grandmas would be looking for their beads, needles, and thread right about now to start sewing beadwork on those bland white robes...

But then it hit me and hit me really hard. It became *my game changer moment!*

I realized that IT HAS NEVER BEEN ABOUT US! It never has been, nor will it ever be! IT IS ALL ABOUT HIM! It is all about Jesus Christ! All glory, honor, and praise is due His Holy name, and He will not share His glory with another!

Isaiah 42:8 hits it home so powerfully;

> *I am the Lord; that is my name! I will not yield my glory to another or my praise to idols.*

How small the petty pursuits of culture seem to be when compared to *the surpassing worth of knowing Christ Jesus my Lord, for whose sake I have lost all things!*

*Passionately pursue Christ,* my indigenous friend, in the time you have remaining here on earth.

*Passionately preach Christ,* pastors, teachers, and missionaries! Do not hesitate to stand on biblical truth with its biblical authority that has been invested in you by God Himself...

...and to all of us, I leave you with these simple and yet profound words...

> *Turn your eyes upon Jesus,*
> *Look full in His wonderful face,*
> *And the things of earth will grow strangely dim,*
> *In the light of His glory and grace.*[59]

Amen and amen!

---

[59] *Turn Your Eyes Upon Jesus,* Helen H. Lemmel, 1922, Public Domain.

CPSIA information can be obtained
at www.ICGtesting.com
Printed in the USA
FSHW011809140619

9 781545 667392